D1067540

Gregg Shorthand

GREGG PUBLISHING DIVISION

Dictionary Simplified

A DICTIONARY OF 30,000 AUTHORITATIVE GREGG SHORTHAND OUTLINES

John Robert Gregg

Louis A. Leslie

Charles E. Zoubek

McGraw-Hill Book Company, Inc.

New York Chicago San Francisco Dallas Toronto London

GREGG SHORTHAND DICTIONARY SIMPLIFIED

Feb. 1960-RD-13

Shorthand Plates Written by

CHARLES RADER

PUBLISHED BY GREGG PUBLISHING DIVISION

McGraw-Hill Book Company, Inc.

Printed in the United States of America

FOREWORD

This shorthand dictionary is divided into three parts:

Part One contains, in alphabetic order, the shorthand outlines for 26,098 words. These 26,098 words, however, represent a considerably larger vocabulary, as many simple derivatives—those ending in *-ing* and *-s,* for example, which present no stenographic problem—have been omitted.

Part Two contains, in alphabetic order, the shorthand outlines for 2,604 entries for personal and geographical names.

Part Three consists of a list of 72 shorthand outlines for abbreviations such as *f.o.b.* and *C.O.D.*

It is easily possible to construct briefer outlines for many of the scientific and literary words for which full outlines are given in this dictionary. It is not advisable to do so, however, unless the writer is certain that he will use those briefer outlines with sufficient frequency to justify the effort of learning them. Otherwise, the brief but half-remembered outline will cause mental hesitation that will result in slower rather than faster writing.

The experience of expert shorthand writers of every system is conclusive in establishing the inadvisability of attempting to gain speed by devising and learning lists of brief outlines. Longer outlines that are quickly constructed by the mind under pressure of dictation give the writer more speed; the attempt to remember and use large numbers of abbreviated outlines tends to reduce the writer's speed.

It is hoped that this volume will render a useful service to the shorthand writer by placing at his disposal a facile and fluent outline for any word in which he may be interested.

The Publishers

PART ONE

Part One of this dictionary contains 26,098 word entries alphabetically arranged.

Experience has proved that those using a shorthand dictionary often consult it for the simple words formerly omitted from shorthand dictionaries or for rare and unusual words likewise formerly omitted.

The present list, therefore, includes many of the apparently simple words formerly omitted. It includes many of the simple derivatives formerly omitted. Most readily apparent will be the addition of the many rare and unusual words that experience has proved are wanted by users of such a list as this.

Many words are included because the shorthand learner, while still in school, has occasion to use them in his schoolwork. For this reason, many mathematical, mineralogical, chemical, physical, botanical, and physiological terms are included. For the same reason, many literary words are included, words that are of no business value but that the high school or college learner uses in schoolwork. The bulk of the vocabulary, however, consists of words used in business-office dictation.

Consistency, rather than brevity of outline, has been the guiding principle in the construction of the shorthand outlines in this *Gregg Shorthand Dictionary Simplified.* The fastest shorthand outline (within reasonable limits) is the outline that requires the least mental effort, the outline that is written consistently and analogically. The speed of a shorthand outline is not to be judged by its brevity to the eye, nor even by its facility for the hand; it is to be judged by the speed with which it may be constructed by the mind and supplied by the mind to the hand.

A

abacus
abaft
abalone
abandon
abandoned
abandonment
abase
abasement
abash
abatable
abate
abated
abatement
abbess
abbey
abbot
abbreviate
abbreviated
abbreviation
abdicate
abdicated
abdication
abdomen
abdominal
abduct
abducted
abduction

abed
aberration
abet
abetted
abettor
abeyance
abhor
abhorred
abhorrence
abhorrent
abide
ability
abject
abjuration
abjure
abjured
ablative
ablaze
able
ablest
ablution
ably
abnegation
abnormal
abnormality
abnormity
aboard

abode
abolish
abolition
abolitionist
abominable
abominate
abomination
aboriginal
aborigines
abortive
abound
aboundingly
about
above
abrade
abraded
abrasion
abrasive
abreast
abridge
abridged
abridgment
abroad
abrogate
abrogated
abrogation
abrupt

abscess
abscissa
abscond
absconded
absconder
absence
absent
absentee
absently
absinth
absolute
absolutely
absolution
absolutism
absolutist
absolve
absorb
absorbed
absorbent
absorbingly
absorption
absorptive
abstain
abstained
abstainer
abstemious
abstemiously
abstemiousness
abstention
abstinence
abstinent

abstract
abstracted
abstractedly
abstraction
abstractly
abstruse
absurd
absurdity
absurdly
abundance
abundant
abuse
abused
abusive
abusively
abusiveness
abut
abutment
abutter
abysm
abysmal
abyss
acacia
academic
academician
academies
academy
Acadian
acanthus
accede
acceded

accelerate
accelerated
acceleration
accelerative
accelerator
accent
accented
accentuate
accentuation
accept
acceptability
acceptable
acceptance
acceptation
access
accessibility
accessible
accession
accessory
accidence
accident
accidental
accidentally
accipitrine
acclaim
acclaimed
acclamation
acclamatory
acclimate
acclimated
acclimation

acclimatization
acclimatize
acclimatized
acclivity
accolade
accommodate
accommodated
accommodatingly
accommodation
accommodative
accompaniment
accompanist
accompany
accomplice
accomplish
accomplished
accomplishment
accord
accordance
accorded
accordingly
accordion
accost
accosted
account
accountability
accountable
accountancy
accountant
accounted
accoutered
accouterment
accredit
accredited
accretion
accrual
accrue
accrued
accumulate
accumulated
accumulates
accumulation
accumulative
accumulator
accuracy
accurate
accurately
accusation
accusative
accuse
accused
accuser
accustom
accustomed
ace
acerb
acerbity
acetate
acetic
acetone
acetylene
ache
achieve
achieved
achievement
achromatic
achromatosis
acid
acidification
acidify
acidity
acidly
acidosis
acidulate
acidulous
acknowledge
acknowledged
acknowledgment
acme
acne
acolyte
aconite
acorn
acoustic
acoustical
acoustics
acquaint
acquaintance
acquaintanceship
acquainted
acquiesce
acquiescence
acquiescent

acquire
acquirement
acquires
acquisition
acquisitive
acquisitiveness
acquit
acquittal
acquitted
acre
acreage
acrid
acridity
acrimonious
acrimoniously
acrimony
acrobat
acrobatic
acropolis
across
acrostic
act
acted
actinic
actinium
action
actionable
activate
active
activities
activity

actor
actress
actual
actualities
actuality
actually
actuary
actuate
actuated
acuity
acumen
acute
acutely
acuteness
adage
adagio
adamant
adamantine
adapt
adaptability
adaptable
adaptation
adapted
adapter
adaptive
add
added
addenda
addendum
adder
addict

addicted
addiction
addition
additional
additionally
additive
address
addressed
addressee
addressograph
adduce
adduct
adduction
adductive
adductor
adenoid
adenology
adenoma
adept
adequacy
adequately
adhere
adhered
adherence
adherent
adhesion
adhesive
adieu
adipose
adjacency
adjacent

adjective
adjoin
adjoined
adjourn
adjourned
adjournment
adjudge
adjudged
adjudicate
adjudicated
adjudication
adjudicator
adjunct
adjuration
adjuratory
adjure
adjured
adjust
adjustable
adjusted
adjuster
adjustment
adjutancy
adjutant
administer
administered
administration
administrative
administratively
administrator
administratrix

admirable
admirably
admiral
admiralty
admiration
admire
admired
admissibility
admissible
admission
admit
admittance
admitted
admittedly
admixture
admonish
admonished
admonition
admonitory
adobe
adolescence
adolescent
adopt
adopted
adoption
adoptive
adorable
adoration
adore
adored
adoringly

adorn
adorned
adornment
adrenal
adrenaline
adrift
adroit
adroitly
adsorption
adulation
adulatory
adult
adulterant
adulterate
adulterated
adulteration
adulterer
adulterous
adultery
adumbrate
adumbration
advance
advanced
advancement
advantage
advantageous
advent
adventitious
adventure
adventurer
adventuresome

adventuress
adventurous
adverb
adverbial
adverbially
adversary
adversative
adverse
adversely
adversity
advert
advertise
advertised
advertisement
advice
advisability
advisable
advisably
advise
advised
advisedly
advisement
advisory
advocacy
advocate
advowson
adz
aegis
Aeolian
aeon
aerate
aerated
aeration
aerial
aerie
aeronautical
affability
affable
affably
affair
affect
affectation
affected
affectedly
affectingly
affection
affectionate
affectionately
affiance
affianced
affiant
affidavit
affiliate
affiliated
affiliation
affinity
affirm
affirmation
affirmative
affirmatory
affirmed
affirmingly
affix
affixed
afflatus
afflict
afflicted
affliction
affluence
affluent
afford
afforded
affray
affright
affront
affronted
afghan
afield
afire
aflame
afloat
afoot
aforementioned
aforesaid
aforetime
afoul
afraid
afresh
after
afterdeck
after-dinner
aftereffect
afterglow

afterlife
aftermath
afternoon
aftertaste
afterthought
afterward
again
against
agape
agate
agateware
agave
age
aged
ageless
agency
agenda
agendum
agent
ageratum
agglomerate
agglomeration
agglomerative
agglutinate
agglutination
agglutinative
aggrandize
aggrandizement
aggravate
aggravated
aggravatingly

aggravation
aggregate
aggregation
aggression
aggressive
aggressor
aggrieved
aghast
agile
agilely
agility
agio
agitate
agitated
agitation
agitator
agnate
agnostic
agnosticism
agonize
agonizingly
agony
agrarian
agree
agreeability
agreeable
agreed
agreement
agricultural
agriculture
agronomy

ague
ahead
ahoy
ahungered
aid
aided
aigrette
aiguillette
ail
ailanthus
ailed
aileron
ailment
aim
aimless
air
aired
airily
airship
airway
airy
aisle
ajar
akimbo
alabaster
alacrity
alamo
alarm
alarmed
alarmingly
alarmist

alas
albatross
albino
album
albumin
albuminous
alchemy
alcohol
alcoholic
alcoholism
alcove
alder
alderman
aldermanic
aleatory
alembic
alert
alertly
alexandrite
alfalfa
algebra
alias
alibi
alien
alienable
alienate
alienation
alienist
alight
alignment
alike

alimentary
alimony
aliquot
alive
alizarin
alkali
alkalinity
all
allay
allegation
allege
alleged
allegedly
allegiance
allegorical
allegory
allergic
allergy
alleviate
alleviated
alleviation
alley
alleyway
alliance
allied
alligator
alliteration
alliterative
alliteratively
allocate
allocated

allocation
allocution
allopath
allopathy
allot
allotment
allotted
allow
allowable
allowance
alloy
alloyed
allspice
allude
alluded
allure
allured
alluringly
allusion
allusive
allusively
alluvial
ally
almanac
almighty
almond
almoner
almost
alms
almshouse
aloe

aloft
aloha
alone
along
aloof
aloofly
alopecia
aloud
alpaca
alphabet
alphabetic
alphabetical
alphabetize
already
also
altar
altarpiece
alter
alterable
alteration
alterative
altercation
alternate
alternated
alternation
alternative
alternator
although
altitude
alto
altogether

altruism
altruist
altruistic
alum
aluminate
aluminum
alumni
alumnus
alveolus
always
alyssum
amalgamate
amalgamated
amalgamation
amanuensis
amaranth
amass
amateur
amateurish
amative
amatory
amaze
amazed
amazingly
Amazon
ambassador
ambassadorial
amber
ambidextrous
ambient
ambiguity

ambiguous
ambition
ambitious
ambitiously
amble
ambrosia
ambrosial
ambulance
ambulatory
ambuscade
ambush
ameliorate
ameliorated
ameliorative
amen
amenable
amend
amended
amendment
amends
amenity
American
Americanization
Americanize
amethyst
amiability
amiable
amicable
amidships
amiss
amity

ammonia
ammonium
ammunition
amnesia
amnesty
amoeba
among
amongst
amorous
amorously
amorphous
amortization
amortize
amortized
amount
amounted
amour
amperage
ampersand
amphibian
amphibious
amphibiously
amphitheater
amphora
ample
amplification
amplifier
amplify
amplitude
amply
ampulla

amputate
amputated
amputation
amuck
amulet
amulets
amuse
amused
amusement
amusingly
anachronism
anachronistic
anachronous
anaconda
anagram
analects
analgesia
analgesic
analogical
analogous
analogy
analysis
analyst
analytic
analytical
analytically
analyze
anarchical
anarchism
anarchist
anarchy

anastigmatic
anathematize
anatomic
anatomical
anatomist
anatomize
anatomy
ancestor
ancestral
ancestry
anchor
anchorage
anchored
anchorite
anchovy
ancient
ancillary
and
andante
andiron
anecdote
anemia
anemometer
anemone
anent
anesthesia
anesthetic
anesthetize
angel
angelic
Angelus

anger
angered
angle
angled
angler
Anglo-Saxon
angrily
angry
anguish
angular
angularity
aniline
animadversion
animal
animate
animated
animatedly
animation
animator
animosity
animus
anise
ankle
anklet
ankylosis
annalist
annals
anneal
annealed
annex
annexation

annihilate
annihilated
annihilation
anniversary
annotate
annotated
annotation
announce
announced
announcement
announcer
annoy
annoyance
annoyed
annoyingly
annual
annually
annuitant
annuity
annul
annular
annulled
annulment
annunciation
annunciator
anode
anodyne
anoint
anointed
anomalies
anomalous

anomaly
anon
anonymity
anonymous
anopheles
another
answer
answerable
answered
ant
antagonism
antagonist
antagonistic
antagonize
antagonized
antarctic
ante
anteater
antecedent
antechamber
antedate
antelope
antenatal
antenna
anterior
anteroom
anthem
anthologist
anthology
anthracite
anthrax

anthropoid
anthropological
anthropology
antic
anticipate
anticipated
anticipation
anticipatory
anticlimax
antidote
antimony
antinomy
antipathy
antiphonal
antipodes
antiquarian
antiquary
antiquated
antique
antiquity
antisepsis
antiseptic
antithesis
antithetical
antitoxin
antler
antlered
antonym
antrum
anvil
anxiety
anxious
any
anybody
anyhow
anyone
anything
anyway
anywhere
aorta
aortic
apart
apartment
apathetic
apathetically
apathy
aperient
aperitive
aperture
apex
aphasia
aphid
aphorism
aphoristic
apiary
apical
apices
apiece
apocalypse
apogee
apologetic
apologetical
apologist
apologize
apologized
apology
apoplectic
apoplexy
apostasy
apostate
apostle
apostolic
apostrophe
apostrophize
apothecary
apothegm
apotheosis
appall
appalled
appallingly
appanage
apparatus
apparel
apparent
apparition
appeal
appealed
appealingly
appear
appearance
appeared
appeasable
appease

appeased
appeasement
appeasingly
appellant
appellate
appellation
appellee
append
appendage
appendectomy
appended
appendicitis
appendix
appendixes
apperceive
apperceived
apperception
apperceptive
appertain
appertained
appetite
appetizer
appetizingly
applaud
applauded
applause
apple
applejack
appliance
applicability
applicable
applicant
application
applicator
applied
apply
appoint
appointed
appointee
appointive
appointment
apportion
apportioned
apportionment
apposite
apposition
appraisal
appraise
appraised
appraisingly
appreciable
appreciably
appreciate
appreciated
appreciation
appreciative
appreciatively
apprehend
apprehended
apprehension
apprehensive
apprentice
apprenticed
apprenticeship
apprise
apprised
approach
approachable
approached
approbation
appropriate
appropriately
appropriateness
appropriation
approval
approve
approved
approvingly
approximate
approximately
approximation
appurtenance
appurtenant
apricot
April
apron
apropos
apse
apt
aptitude
aptly
aptness
aquamarine

aquarium
aquatic
aqueduct
aqueous
aquiline
Arab
arabesque
Arabian
Arabic
arable
arbiter
arbitrage
arbitrament
arbitrarily
arbitrariness
arbitrary
arbitrated
arbitration
arbitrator
arbor
arboreal
arboretum
arbutus
arc
arcade
arcanum
arch
archaic
archangel
archbishop
archdeacon
archduchess
archduchy
archduke
archeology
archer
archery
archetype
archipelago
architect
architectonic
architectural
archives
archivist
archly
archway
arctic
ardent
ardently
ardor
arduous
arduously
are
area
arena
argent
argentiferous
argon
Argonaut
arguable
argue
argument
argumentation
argumentative
argyrol
arid
aridity
arise
aristocracy
aristocrat
aristocratic
arithmetic
arithmetical
ark
arm
armada
armadillo
armament
armature
armchair
armed
Armenian
armful
armistice
armlet
armor
armorial
armory
armpit
armscye
army
arnica
aroma

aromatic
arouse
arpeggio
arraign
arraignment
arrange
arranged
arrangement
arras
array
arrearage
arrears
arrest
arrival
arrive
arrogance
arrogant
arrogate
arrowhead
arrowy
arroyo
arsenal
arsenate
arsenic
arsenical
arsenide
arsenite
arson
art
arterial
artery

artful
artfully
arthritis
artichoke
article
articulate
articulated
articulation
artifact
artifice
artificial
artificiality
artificially
artillery
artist
artistic
artistry
artless
Aryan
as
asbestos
ascend
ascendant
ascendency
ascension
ascent
ascertain
ascertainment
ascetic
asceticism
ascorbic

ascribe
ascribed
ascription
asepsis
aseptic
ash
ashamed
ashen
ashes
ashlar
ashore
ashy
Asiatic
aside
asinine
ask
askance
askew
aslant
asleep
asp
asparagus
aspect
aspen
asperity
aspersion
asphalt
asphodel
asphyxiate
asphyxiation
aspic

aspirant
aspirate
aspiration
aspire
aspired
aspirin
assagai
assailant
assassin
assassinate
assassinated
assassination
assault
assaulted
assay
assayed
assemblage
assemble
assembly
assent
assented
assentingly
assert
asserted
assertion
assertive
assertively
assess
assessable
assessed
assessment

assessor
asset
asseverate
asseveration
assiduity
assiduous
assiduously
assign
assignable
assigned
assignee
assignment
assignor
assimilate
assimilated
assimilation
assist
assistance
assistant
assisted
assists
associate
associated
association
associative
assorted
assortment
assuage
assuaged
assumably
assume

assumed
assumpsit
assumption
assurance
assure
assured
assuredly
Assyrian
aster
asterisk
astern
asteroid
asthenia
asthma
asthmatic
astigmatic
astigmatism
astonish
astonishingly
astonishment
astound
astoundingly
astragalus
astrakhan
astral
astray
astride
astringency
astringent
astrologer
astrology

astronomer
astronomical
astronomy
astute
astutely
astuteness
asunder
asylum
asymmetric
asymmetrical
at
atavism
atheism
atheist
atheistic
atheneum
Athenian
athlete
athletic
athletics
athwart
atmosphere
atmospheric
atoll
atom
atomic
atomize
atomized
atomizer
atone
atoned

atonement
atrium
atrocious
atrociously
atrocity
atrophied
atrophy
atropine
attach
attached
attachment
attack
attacker
attain
attainable
attainder
attained
attainment
attar
attempt
attempted
attend
attendance
attendant
attention
attentive
attentively
attentiveness
attenuate
attenuated
attenuation

attest
attestation
attests
attic
attire
attired
attitude
attitudinize
attorney
attract
attracted
attraction
attractive
attractively
attribute
attribution
attributive
attrition
auburn
auction
auctioneer
audacious
audaciously
audacity
audibility
audible
audibly
audience
audit
audited
audition

auditor
auditorium
auditory
auger
aught
augment
augmentation
augmentative
augur
augured
augury
august
August
augustly
auk
aunt
aura
aureole
auricle
auricular
auriferous
aurora
auroral
auscultate
auscultation
auspices
auspicious
austere
austerely
austerity
Australian
Austrian
authentic
authenticate
authentication
authenticity
author
authoritarian
authoritative
authority
authorization
authorize
authorized
authorship
autobiography
autochthonous
autocracy
autocrat
autocratic
autograph
automatic
automatism
automaton
automobile
autonomous
autonomy
autopsy
autosuggestion
autumn
autumnal
auxiliary
avail
availability
available
availed
avalanche
avarice
avaricious
avariciously
avatar
avenge
avenged
avenue
aver
average
averred
averse
aversion
avert
averted
aviary
aviation
aviator
avid
avidity
avidly
avigation
avocado
avocation
avoid
avoidable
avowal
avowedly

avuncular	awash	awoke
await	away	ax
awaited	awestricken	axiom
awake	awestruck	axiomatic
awaken	awful	axis
awakened	awkward	axle
award	awkwardly	azalea
awarded	awkwardness	azimuth
aware	awl	azure
awareness	awning	azurite

B

babbitt
baboon
baby
baccalaureate
bacchanal
bachelor
bachelorhood
back
backboard
backbone
backer
backfire
backgammon
background
backhand
backhanded
backlash
backlog
backslide
backwardness
backwash
backwater
bacon
bacteria
bacterial
bacteriological
bacteriology

bad
badger
badinage
badly
badminton
badness
baffle
baffled
bag
bagged
bagasse
bagatelle
baggage
bagpipe
bail
bailed
bailiff
bailiwick
bailment
bait
baize
bake
bakelite
baker
bakery
balance
balbriggan

balcony
bald
baldachin
baldric
bale
baled
baleful
balk
ball
ballad
ballast
ballerina
ballet
ballistics
balloon
balloonist
ballot
ballroom
balm
balsam
balsamiferous
baluster
balustrade
bamboo
bamboozle
bamboozled
ban

banal
banality
banana
band
bandage
bandanna
bandbox
bandeau
banded
bandit
banditti
bandmaster
bandoleer
bandy
baneful
bang
bangboard
banged
bangle
banish
banishment
banister
banjo
bank
bankbook
banked
banker
bankrupt
bankruptcy
banned
banner

banquet
banshee
bantam
banter
bantered
banteringly
banyan
baptism
baptismal
Baptist
baptize
baptized
bar
barb
barbarian
barbaric
barbarism
barbarity
barbarous
barbecue
barbed
barber
barberry
barbican
bard
bare
bareback
bared
barefaced
bareheaded
barely

bareness
bargain
bargained
barge
bargeman
baritone
barium
bark
barley
barn
barnacle
barogram
barograph
barometer
barometric
baron
baroness
baronet
baronetcy
baronial
baroque
barrack
barracuda
barrage
barratry
barrel
barren
barrenness
barricade
barrier
barrister

barrow
barter
bartered
basal
bascule
base
baseboard
baseless
basely
baseman
basement
baseness
baser
basest
bashful
basic
basically
basilica
basilisk
basin
basis
bask
basket
bas-relief
bass
bassinet
basso
bassoon
basswood
baste
bastinado

bastion
bat
batch
bateau
bath
bather
bathhouse
bathos
baton
battalion
batter
battered
battery
battle
battled
battleship
bawl
bawled
bayberry
bayonet
bayou
bazaar
be
beach
beacon
bead
beaded
beadle
beadwork
beagle
beak

beaker
beam
beamed
bean
bear
bearable
beard
bearded
bearskin
beast
beastliness
beastly
beat
beaten
beater
beatific
beatification
beatify
beatings
beatitude
beau
beauteous
beautiful
beautifully
beautify
beauty
beaver
becalm
became
because
beckon

beckoned
becloud
become
becomingly
bed
bedbug
bedchamber
bedeck
bedevil
bedfellow
bedizen
bedlam
bedpost
bedridden
bedroom
bedside
bedspread
bedspring
bedstead
bedtime
bee
beech
beef
beefsteak
beer
beeswax
beetle
befall
befit
befog
before

beforehand
befriend
befuddle
beg
beget
beggar
begged
begin
begone
begonia
begot
begrime
beguile
beguiled
begun
behalf
behave
behavior
behead
beheadings
beheld
behemoth
behest
behind
behold
beholden
beholder
beige
bejewel
belch
beleaguered

belfry
Belgian
belie
belief
believable
believe
belittle
belittled
belittlingly
bell
belladonna
bellboy
bellicose
bellicosity
belligerence
belligerency
belligerent
belligerently
bellows
belong
belonged
belongings
beloved
below
belt
belted
belvedere
bemused
bench
bend
bended

beneath
benediction
benefaction
benefactor
benefactress
benefice
beneficence
beneficent
beneficial
beneficiary
benefit
benevolence
benevolent
benighted
benignancy
benignant
benignity
bent
benzene
bequeath
bequest
bereave
bereaved
berry
berth
beryl
beseech
beseeched
beseechingly
beset
beside

besides
besiege
bespangle
bespeak
Bessemer
best
bestial
bestiality
bestow
bestowed
bestride
bet
betake
betimes
betrayal
betrayer
betroth
betrothal
better
bettered
betterment
between
betwixt
bevel
beveled
beverage
bevy
bewail
bewailed
beware
bewilder

bewildered
bewilderment
bewitch
beyond
bezel
biannual
biannually
bias
biased
bibelot
Bible
Biblical
bibliographical
bibliography
bibulous
bicameral
bicarbonate
bicentenary
biceps
bichloride
bichromate
bicuspid
bicycle
bid
bidder
bide
biennial
bier
bifocal
big
bigamist

bigamous	bimetallist	birthright
bigamy	bimonthly	biscuit
bigger	binary	bisect
biggest	binder	bishop
bighorn	bindery	bishopric
bight	bindingly	bismuth
bigot	bindings	bison
bigoted	bindweed	bisque
bigotry	binnacle	bit
bijou	binocular	bite
bilateral	binomial	biter
bile	biographer	bitingly
bilge	biographic	bitten
biliary	biographical	bitter
bilingual	biographically	bitterly
bilious	biography	bittern
bilk	biological	bitterness
bill	biologically	bitters
billboard	biologist	bitumen
billed	biology	bituminous
billhead	biopsy	bivouac
billiards	biplane	bizarre
billings	bipolar	black
billion	birch	blackball
billionaire	bird	blackberry
billow	birdlime	blackbird
billowy	birdman	blackboard
billposter	birth	blacken
billsticker	birthday	blacker
bimetallic	birthmark	blackest
bimetallism	birthplace	blackfish

blackhead
blackish
blackjack
blackmail
blackness
blacksmith
bladder
blade
blame
blamed
blameless
blameworthy
blanch
bland
blandish
blandly
blandness
blank
blanker
blankest
blanket
blankly
blare
blared
blarney
blaspheme
blasphemed
blasphemous
blasphemy
blast
blasted

blatant
blaze
blazer
blazon
bleach
bleacher
bleak
bleat
bleed
blemish
blench
blend
blended
blendings
bless
blessedness
blessings
blew
blight
blimp
blind
blinded
blinder
blindfold
blindly
blink
blinker
bliss
blissful
blissfully
blister

blistered
blisteringly
blistery
blithe
blithely
blithesome
blizzard
bloat
block
blockade
blockhead
blockhouse
blond
blood
blooded
bloodier
bloodiest
bloodless
bloodletting
bloodroot
bloodshed
bloodshot
bloodstain
bloody
bloom
bloomed
bloomer
blossom
blossomed
blot
blotch

blotter
blouse
blow
blower
blowfish
blowgun
blowhole
blown
blowpipe
blowtorch
blowy
blubber
bludgeon
blue
bluefish
bluestocking
bluff
blunder
blunderbuss
blundered
blunderingly
blunt
blunted
bluntly
bluntness
blur
blurred
blurt
blush
blushingly
bluster

blustered
blusteringly
boa
boar
board
boarded
boarder
boast
boaster
boastful
boastfully
boat
boatswain
bobbin
bobolink
bobtail
bode
bodice
bodily
bodkin
body
bog
boggle
boggled
bogus
Bohemian
boil
boiled
boiler
boisterous
boisterously

bola
bold
boldly
boldness
bolero
boll
bolo
bolometer
bolster
bolstered
bolt
bolted
bolthead
bolus
bomb
bombard
bombarded
bombardier
bombardment
bombast
bombastic
bomber
bombings
bombproof
bombshell
bonanza
bonbon
bond
bondage
bonded
bondholder

bondman
bondsman
bone
boned
boneless
boneset
bonfire
bonito
bonnet
bonus
booby
boodle
book
bookbinder
bookings
bookish
bookkeeper
bookkeeping
booklet
booklets
bookmaker
bookmark
bookplate
bookrack
bookseller
bookshelf
bookshop
bookstore
bookworm
boom
boomed
boomerang
boon
boorish
boost
boosted
booster
boot
bootblack
booted
bootee
booth
bootjack
bootleg
bootlegger
bootless
booty
booze
boracic
borate
borax
Bordeaux
border
bordered
bore
bored
boredom
borer
boric
borings
born
boron
borough
borrow
borrowed
borrowings
bosky
bosom
boss
botanic
botanical
botanist
botanize
botany
botch
both
bother
bothersome
bottle
bottled
bottom
bottomless
bottomry
botulism
boudoir
bough
bought
boulder
boulevard
bounce
bouncer
bound
boundary

bounded	boysenberry	brave
bounden	brace	braver
boundless	bracelet	bravery
bounteous	bracelets	bravest
bounteously	bracket	bravo
bountiful	bracketed	brawl
bounty	brackish	brawler
bouquet	bradawl	brawny
bourgeois	brag	brazen
bout	braid	brazier
bovine	braided	breach
bow	Braille	bread
bow	brain	breadfruit
bower	brainless	breadth
bowknot	brainy	breadwinner
bowl	braise	break
bowlder	brake	breakable
bowled	brakeman	breakage
bowlegged	bramble	breakdown
bowman	bran	breakfast
bowshot	branch	breakneck
bowsprit	brand	breakwater
box	branded	breast
boxed	brandied	breastbone
boxer	brandish	breastpin
boxwood	brandy	breastplate
boy	brash	breastwork
boycott	brass	breath
boyhood	brassard	breathless
boyish	brassy	breech
boyishness	bravado	breed

breeder
breeze
brethren
breve
brevet
breviary
brevier
brevity
brew
brewery
bribe
bribed
bribery
brick
brickbat
bricklayer
brickyard
bridal
bride
bridge
bridgehead
bridle
bridled
brief
briefer
briefest
briefly
brier
brig
brigade
brigadier

brigand
brigandage
brigantine
bright
brighten
brighter
brightest
brightly
brightness
brilliance
brilliant
brilliantly
brim
brimful
brimstone
brindled
brine
bring
brink
briny
briquette
brisk
brisket
bristle
bristled
bristly
Britannia
Britannic
British
Britisher
Briton

brittle
brittleness
broach
broad
broadcast
broaden
broader
broadest
broadloom
broadly
broadside
brocade
brocatel
broccoli
brochette
brochure
brogan
brogue
broil
broiled
broiler
broke
broken
brokenly
broker
brokerage
bromate
bromide
bromine
bronchial
bronchitis

bronze
brood
brooded
brooder
brook
brooklet
brooklets
broom
broth
brother
brotherhood
brother-in-law
brotherly
brougham
brought
brow
brown
browse
bruin
bruise
bruised
bruit
brunette
brunt
brush
brushwood
brusque
brutal
brutality
brutalize
brutally

brute
brutish
bubble
bubonic
buccal
buccaneer
buck
buckboard
bucket
bucketful
buckle
buckled
buckler
buckram
bucksaw
buckshot
buckskin
buckwheat
bucolic
bud
budge
budged
budget
budgetary
buff
buffalo
buffer
buffoon
buffoonery
bug
bugbear

bugle
bugler
build
builder
buildings
built
bulb
bulbous
bulge
bulged
bulk
bulkhead
bulkiest
bulky
bull
bullet
bulletin
bullfight
bullfinch
bullfrog
bullhead
bullion
bullish
bullock
bully
bullyrag
bulrush
bulwark
bum
bumboat
bump

bumper
bumpier
bumpiest
bumpkin
bumpy
buna
bunch
bundle
bundled
bung
bungalow
bungle
bungled
bungler
bunion
bunker
buoy
buoyant
buoyantly
burden
burdensome
bureau
bureaucracy
bureaucrat
burette
burgee
burgeon
burgess
burglar
burglary
burial

burin
burlap
burlesque
burly
burn
burned
burner
burnish
burnt
burr
burro
burrow
bursar
burst
bury
bus
bush
bushings
busily
business
businesslike
buskin
bust
bustard
bustle
bustled
busy
busybody
but
butcher
butchery

butler
butt
butter
butterball
buttercup
buttered
butterfat
butterfly
butternut
butterscotch
buttery
button
buttonhole
buttonholed
buttress
buxom
buy
buyer
buzz
buzzard
buzzer
by
bygone
bypass
bypath
byplay
by-product
Byronic
bystander
byway
byword

C

cab
cabal
cabbage
cabin
cabinet
cable
cablegram
caboose
cacao
cachalot
cache
cachet
cackle
cackled
cactus
cadaver
cadaverous
caddie
cadence
cadenza
cadet
cadmium
Cadmus
cadre
caduceus
cafe
cafeteria

caffeine
cage
caged
cairn
caitiff
cajole
cajolery
cake
cakewalk
calabash
calamitous
calamitously
calamity
calcification
calcify
calcimine
calcine
calcined
calcium
calculate
calculated
calculation
calculator
caldron
calendar
calf
calfskin

caliber
calibrate
calibration
calico
caliper
calisthenics
calk
call
calla
called
caller
calligraphy
calliope
callosity
callous
calloused
callously
callow
callowly
callus
calm
calmer
calmest
calmly
calmness
calomel
caloric

calorie
calumniate
calumniated
calumniation
calumniator
calumny
Calvary
calved
calyx
camber
cambium
cambric
came
camel
cameleer
Camelot
cameo
camera
camomile
camouflage
camp
campaign
campanile
camper
camphor
camphorate
campus
can
canal
canary
cancel
canceled
cancellation
cancer
cancerous
candelabrum
candid
candidacy
candidate
candidly
candied
candle
candled
candlefish
candlelight
candlenut
candlestick
candor
candy
cane
canine
canister
canker
cankerous
cannery
cannibal
cannibalism
cannily
cannon
cannonade
cannoneer
canny
canoe
canon
canonical
canonicals
canonize
canopy
can't
cant
cantaloupe
cantankerous
cantata
canteen
canter
canticle
cantilever
cantle
canto
canton
cantor
canvas
caoutchouc
capabilities
capability
capable
capably
capacious
capacitate
capacitated
capacity
cape
caper

caperings
capillarity
capillary
capital
capitalism
capitalist
capitalists
capitalization
capitalize
capitalized
capitulate
capitulated
capitulates
capitulation
caprice
capricious
capsize
capstan
capsule
captain
captaincy
caption
captious
captiously
captiousness
captivate
captivated
captivation
captive
captivity
capture
captured
car
carabineer
caracole
caracoled
carafe
caramel
caramelize
carapace
carat
caravan
caravansary
caravel
caraway
carbide
carbine
carbohydrate
carbolic
carbon
carbonate
carbonic
carboniferous
carbonize
carbonized
carborundum
carboy
carbuncle
carburetor
carcass
carcinoma
card
cardboard
cardiac
cardinal
cardiograph
cardiology
carditis
care
cared
careen
careened
career
careful
carefully
carefulness
careless
carelessly
carelessness
caress
caressingly
caret
carfare
cargo
caribou
caricature
caricatured
caries
carillon
carminative
carmine
carnage
carnal

carnally
carnation
carnelian
carnival
carnivorous
carol
caroled
carom
caromed
carotid
carouse
caroused
carp
carpal
carpenter
carpet
carpeted
carriage
carrier
carrion
carrot
carrousel
carry
cart
cartage
carted
cartel
cartilage
cartilaginous
cartography
carton

cartoon
cartouche
cartridge
carve
carved
carver
caryatid
cascade
case
casein
casement
cash
cashed
cashier
cashmere
casino
cask
casket
cassation
cassava
casserole
cassia
cassock
cast
castanet
caste
caster
castigate
castigated
castigation
castle

castoff
castor
castrametation
casual
casually
casualty
casuist
casuistry
cataclysm
catacomb
catafalque
Catalan
catalepsy
cataleptic
catalogue
catalpa
catalysis
catalytic
catalyze
catamount
catapult
cataract
catarrh
catarrhal
catastrophe
catastrophic
Catawba
catbird
catboat
catch
catcher

catchword
catchy
catechism
catechize
categorical
category
catenary
cater
catered
caterer
caterpillar
catfish
catgut
cathedral
catheter
catheterize
cathode
catholic
catholicism
catholicity
catnip
cattle
caucus
caudal
caught
causal
causality
causation
causative
cause
causeless

causeway
caustic
cauterization
cauterize
cauterized
cautery
caution
cautionary
cautious
cavalcade
cavalier
cavalry
cave
caveat
cavern
cavernous
caviar
cavil
cavity
cavort
cayenne
cease
ceased
ceaseless
cecum
cedar
cede
ceded
cedilla
ceilings
celebrant

celebrate
celebrated
celebration
celebrity
celerity
celery
celesta
celestial
celestially
celibacy
celibate
cell
cellar
cellarer
cellaret
cellist
cello
cellophane
cellular
cellulitis
celluloid
cellulose
Celtic
cement
cementation
cemetery
cenobite
cenotaph
censer
censor
censorial

censorious
censorship
censurable
censure
censured
census
cent
centaur
centenarian
centenary
centennial
center
centerboard
centered
centerpiece
centigrade
centimeter
centipede
central
centralization
centralize
centralized
centrally
centrifugal
centripetal
century
cephalalgia
cephalic
ceramic
cereal
cerebellum
cerebral
cerebrum
cerement
ceremonial
ceremonially
ceremonious
ceremoniously
ceremoniousness
ceremony
cerise
cerium
certain
certainly
certainty
certificate
certification
certify
certiorari
certitude
cervical
cervix
cesium
cessation
cession
cesspool
cestus
cetacean
chafe
chaffinch
chagrin
chain
chained
chainwork
chair
chairman
chaise
chalcedony
chalet
chalice
chalk
chalkiness
challenge
challenged
chamber
chambered
chamberlain
chambermaid
chameleon
chamois
champagne
champion
championship
chance
chanced
chancel
chancellery
chancellor
chancery
chandelier
chandler
chandlery
change

changeable
changeless
changeling
channel
channeled
chant
chanted
chaos
chaotic
chapel
chaperon
chaplain
chaplet
chaplets
chapter
chapters
char
character
characteristic
characteristically
characterization
characterize
characterized
charade
charcoal
chard
charge
chargeable
charged
charger
chariot

charioteer
charitable
charitably
charity
charlatan
charm
charmed
charmingly
chart
charted
charter
chartreuse
chary
chase
chasm
chassis
chaste
chasten
chastened
chasteningly
chastise
chastised
chastisement
chastity
chasuble
chateau
chatelaine
chattel
chatter
chattered
chatterer

chatty
cheap
cheapen
cheapened
cheaper
cheapest
cheaply
cheapness
cheat
cheated
check
checked
checker
checkerboard
checkered
checkmate
checkrein
cheeky
cheer
cheered
cheerful
cheerfully
cheerfulness
cheerily
cheeringly
cheerless
cheerlessly
cheery
cheese
cheesecake
cheesecloth

chef
chemical
chemically
chemise
chemist
chemistry
chemurgy
chenille
cherish
cheroot
cherry
cherub
chess
chest
chestnut
chevron
chew
chicanery
chicken
chicle
chicory
chide
chief
chiefly
chieftain
chiffon
chiffonier
chilblain
child
childhood
childish
childishly
childishness
childless
childlike
children
chili
chill
chilled
chillier
chilliest
chillingly
chilly
chime
chimed
chimera
chimerical
chimney
chimpanzee
chin
china
chinch
chinchilla
chine
Chinese
chink
chintz
chip
chipmunk
chipper
chirography
chiropodist
chirp
chisel
chiseled
chitterling
chivalric
chivalrous
chivalry
chive
chloral
chlorate
chloride
chlorinate
chlorine
chlorite
chloroform
chlorophyll
chlorosis
chocolate
choice
choir
choke
choler
cholera
choleric
choose
chop
chophouse
choral
chord
chorea
chortle

chorus
chose
chosen
chowder
chrism
christen
Christendom
christened
christenings
Christian
Christianity
Christmas
chromatics
chrome
chromium
chronic
chronicle
chronicled
chronicles
chronological
chronologically
chronology
chronometer
chrysalis
chrysanthemum
chubbiness
chubby
chuck
chuckle
chucklehead
chum

chummy
chump
chunk
church
churchman
churlish
churlishly
churn
churned
chute
chutney
cicada
cicatrix
cicatrize
cider
cigar
cigarette
cinch
cincture
cinder
cinematograph
cinnamon
cinquefoil
cion
cipher
circle
circled
circuit
circuitous
circuitously
circuitousness

circular
circularize
circulate
circulated
circulation
circulatory
circumambient
circumference
circumferential
circumflex
circumlocution
circumlocutory
circumnavigate
circumscribe
circumscribed
circumspect
circumspection
circumspectly
circumspectness
circumstance
circumstances
circumstantial
circumstantially
circumstantiate
circumvent
circumvention
circus
cirrhosis
cirrhotic
cistern
citadel

citation
cite
cited
citizen
citizenry
citizenship
citrate
citric
citron
city
civic
civil
civilian
civility
civilization
civilize
civilized
claim
claimant
claimed
clairvoyance
clairvoyant
clamant
clambake
clamber
clambered
clammy
clamor
clamored
clamorous
clamp

clamshell
clan
clandestine
clang
clanged
clangor
clank
clanked
clap
clapper
claptrap
claque
claret
clarification
clarify
clarinet
clarion
clarity
clash
clasp
class
classic
classical
classicism
classicist
classicists
classification
classify
classmate
clatter
clattered

clause
claustrophobia
clavichord
clavicle
claw
clay
clean
cleaned
cleaner
cleanest
cleanliness
cleanly
cleanness
cleanse
cleanser
clear
clearance
cleared
clearer
clearest
clearly
clearness
cleat
cleavage
cleave
cleaver
clef
cleft
clematis
clemency
clement

clench	clinker	cloudy
clerestory	clip	clove
clergy	clipper	cloven
clergyman	clippings	clover
clerical	clique	clown
clerk	cloak	clowned
clever	clock	clownish
cleverer	clockwise	cloy
cleverest	clod	cloyed
cleverly	clog	club
cleverness	cloister	cluck
clew	cloistered	clump
click	clonic	clumsier
client	close	clumsiest
clientele	closed	clumsily
cliff	closely	clumsiness
climacteric	closeness	clumsy
climate	closer	cluster
climatic	closest	clustered
climax	closet	clutch
climb	closure	clutter
climbed	clot	cluttered
climber	clothe	coach
clinch	clothes	coachman
clincher	clothespin	coadjutor
cling	clothier	coagulate
clingingly	clotted	coagulated
clinic	cloud	coagulates
clinical	cloudiness	coagulation
clinician	cloudless	coagulative
clink	clouds	coal

coalesce
coalescence
coalescent
coalition
coalsack
coarse
coarsen
coarsened
coarser
coarsest
coast
coastal
coaster
coastwise
coat
coatings
coauthor
coax
coaxed
coaxial
coaxingly
cobalt
cobble
cobra
cobweb
cocaine
coccyx
cochineal
cockade
cockatoo
cockney

cockpit
cockroach
cocksure
cocksureness
cocktail
cocoa
cocoon
code
coded
codefendant
codeine
codex
codfish
codicil
codification
codify
coeducation
coefficient
coerce
coerced
coercion
coercive
coeval
coexecutor
coffee
coffer
coffin
cogency
cogent
cogitate
cogitated

cogitation
cogitative
cognac
cognate
cognizance
cognizant
cognomen
cohabit
cohere
cohered
coherence
coherent
coherently
coherer
cohesion
cohesive
cohesiveness
cohort
coif
coiffure
coign
coil
coiled
coin
coinage
coincide
coincidence
coincidental
coined
coiner
coinsurance

coinsure	collision	columbine
coinsurer	collocation	column
coke	collodion	columnar
colander	colloid	coma
cold	colloidal	comatose
colder	colloquial	comb
coldest	colloquy	combat
coldly	collotype	combatant
colic	collusion	combative
colitis	collusive	combed
collaborate	cologne	combination
collaboration	colon	combine
collapse	colonel	combings
collar	colonial	combust
collate	colonist	combustible
collated	colonization	combustion
collateral	colonize	come
collation	colonized	comedian
colleague	colonnade	comedy
collect	colony	comeliness
collected	colophon	comely
collectible	color	comestible
collection	coloration	comet
collective	colored	comfit
collector	colorings	comfort
college	colorless	comfortable
collegiate	colossal	comfortably
collide	Colosseum	comforted
collided	colossus	comforter
collie	colporteur	comic
collier	colt	comical

comings
comma
command
commandeer
commander
commandingly
commandment
commando
commemorate
commemorated
commemoration
commemorative
commence
commenced
commencement
commend
commendable
commendation
commendatory
commended
commensurable
commensurate
comment
commentary
commentator
commented
commerce
commercial
commercialism
commercialization
commercialize

comminatory
commingle
commingled
comminute
comminuted
comminution
commiserate
commiseration
commissariat
commissary
commission
commissioned
commissioner
commit
commitment
committed
committee
commodious
commodity
commodore
common
commonalty
commoner
commonest
commonly
commonplace
commonwealth
commotion
communal
commune
communicable

communicant
communicate
communication
communicative
communion
communism
communist
communistic
community
communize
commutation
commutator
commute
commuted
commuter
compact
companion
companionable
companionship
companionway
company
comparability
comparable
comparative
compare
compared
comparison
compartment
compass
compassion
compassionate

compassionately
compatible
compatriot
compeer
compel
compelled
compellingly
compend
compendious
compendium
compensate
compensation
compensatory
compete
competence
competent
competently
competition
competitive
competitor
compilation
compile
compiled
complacence
complacency
complacent
complain
complainant
complained
complainingly
complaint

complaisant
complement
complemental
complementary
complemented
complete
completed
completion
complex
complexion
complexity
compliance
compliant
complicate
complicated
complication
complicity
complied
compliment
complimentary
complin
comply
component
comport
compose
composed
composer
composite
composition
compositor
compost

composure
compote
compound
comprehend
comprehended
comprehensibility
comprehensible
comprehension
comprehensive
compress
compressibility
compressible
compression
compressor
comprise
compromise
compromisingly
comptometer
comptroller
compulsion
compulsory
compunction
computation
compute
computed
comrade
concatenation
concave
concavity
conceal
concealed

concealment
concede
conceit
conceited
conceitedly
conceivable
conceivably
conceive
conceived
concentrate
concentration
concentric
concept
conception
conceptual
concern
concerned
concert
concerted
concertina
concession
concessionaire
conch
conciliate
conciliated
conciliation
conciliatory
concise
concisely
conciseness
conclave

conclude
concluded
conclusion
conclusive
conclusively
concoct
concoction
concomitant
concord
concordance
concourse
concrete
concur
concurred
concurrence
concurrent
concussion
condemn
condemnation
condemnatory
condemned
condensation
condense
condensed
condenser
condescend
condescendingly
condescension
condign
condiment
condition

conditional
conditionally
condole
condolence
condonation
condone
condoned
condor
conducive
conduct
conducted
conduction
conductivity
conductor
conduit
condyle
cone
confection
confectioner
confectionery
confederacy
confederate
confederation
confer
conferee
conference
conferred
confess
confessedly
confession
confessional

confessor
confide
confided
confidence
confident
confidential
confidentially
confidently
confidingly
configuration
confine
confined
confinement
confirm
confirmation
confirmed
confiscate
confiscated
confiscation
confiscatory
conflagration
conflict
confliction
confluence
confluent
conform
conformable
conformation
conformed
conformer
conformity
confound
confounded
confrere
confront
confrontation
confronted
confuse
confused
confusedly
confusingly
confusion
confutation
confute
confuted
congeal
congealed
congenial
congeniality
congenially
congenital
congest
congestion
conglomerate
conglomeration
congratulate
congratulated
congratulates
congratulation
congratulatory
congregate
congregated
congregation
congregational
congress
congressional
congruence
congruent
congruity
congruous
conic
conical
coniferous
conjectural
conjecture
conjectured
conjugal
conjugate
conjugated
conjugation
conjunction
conjunctive
conjunctivitis
conjuration
conjure
conjured
conjurer
connect
connectedly
connecter
connection
connective
connivance

connive
connoisseur
connotation
connote
connubial
conquer
conquered
conqueror
conquest
conquests
consanguinity
conscience
conscientious
conscientiously
conscious
consciously
consciousness
conscript
consecrate
consecrated
consecration
consecutive
consensus
consent
consented
consequence
consequent
consequential
consequently
conservation
conservatism
conservative
conservatory
conserve
conserved
consider
considerable
considerate
consideration
considers
consign
consigned
consignee
consignment
consignor
consist
consistency
consistent
consistory
consists
consolation
console
consoled
consolidate
consolidated
consolidation
consolingly
consols
consonance
consonant
consonantal
consort
consorted
conspicuous
conspicuously
conspiracy
conspirator
conspiratorial
conspire
conspired
constable
constabulary
constancy
constant
constantly
constellation
consternation
constipation
constituency
constituent
constitute
constituted
constitution
constitutional
constitutionality
constitutionally
constrain
constrained
constraint
constrict
constriction
construct
constructed

constructive
construe
construed
consul
consular
consulate
consulates
consult
consultant
consultation
consultative
consulted
consumable
consume
consummate
consummation
consumption
consumptive
contact
contagion
contagious
contain
contained
container
contaminate
contamination
contemplate
contemplation
contemporaneous
contemporary
contempt

contemptible
contemptuous
contend
contended
contender
content
contented
contention
contentious
contentment
contest
contestant
contestation
contests
context
contextual
contiguity
contiguous
continence
continent
continental
contingency
contingent
continual
continually
continuance
continuant
continuation
continue
continued
continuity

continuous
continuously
continuum
contort
contorted
contortion
contortionist
contour
contraband
contrabass
contract
contracted
contractile
contraction
contractor
contradict
contradiction
contradictory
contradis-
tinction
contraindicate
contralto
contraption
contrary
contrast
contrasts
contravene
contravention
contribute
contribution
contributor
contributory

contrite
contritely
contrition
contrivance
contrive
control
controllable
controlled
controller
controversial
controversy
controvert
contumacious
contumacy
contumely
contuse
contusion
conundrum
convalesce
convalescence
convalescent
convection
convene
convened
convenience
conveniences
convenient
conveniently
convent
convention
conventional

conventionality
conventionalize
conventionally
conventual
converge
convergence
convergent
conversant
conversation
conversational
conversationalist
converse
conversion
convert
converted
convertibility
convertible
convex
convexity
convey
conveyance
conveyed
conveyor
convict
convicted
conviction
convince
convincingly
convivial
conviviality
convivially

convocation
convoke
convoked
convolution
convoy
convoyed
convulse
convulsion
convulsive
cooker
cookery
cool
cooled
cooler
coolest
coolie
coolly
coolness
coop
cooper
cooperage
co-operate
co-operation
co-operative
co-opt
co-ordinate
co-ordination
copartner
copartnership
Copernican
copious

copiously	cornered	corresponds
copiousness	cornice	corridor
copper	cornucopia	corroborate
copperhead	corona	corroboration
copperplate	coroner	corroborative
coppersmith	coronet	corroboratory
copra	corporal	corrode
copy	corporate	corroded
copyright	corporately	corrosion
coracle	corporation	corrosive
coral	corporeal	corrugate
cord	corps	corrugation
cordage	corpse	corrupt
corded	corpulence	corrupted
cordial	corpulent	corruptible
cordiality	corpuscle	corruption
cordially	corpuscular	corruptly
cordite	corral	corsage
cordon	correct	corsair
Cordovan	correction	corset
corduroy	corrective	cortege
core	correctly	cortex
cored	correctness	cortical
corespondent	corrector	corundum
Corinthian	correlate	coruscate
cork	correlation	coruscation
corkscrew	correlative	coryza
cormorant	correspond	cosily
corn	correspondence	cosine
cornea	correspondent	cosiness
corner	correspondingly	cosmetic

cosmic
cosmopolitan
cosmos
Cossack
cost
costliness
costly
costume
costumer
coterie
cottage
cotter
cotton
cottontail
couch
cougar
cough
could
council
councilor
counsel
counseled
count
counted
countenance
counter
counteract
counterbalance
countercharge
countercheck
countered

counterfeit
counterfeiter
counterirritant
countermand
countermine
counterpart
counterplot
counterpoint
countershaft
countersign
countersink
counterweight
countess
countless
country
county
coupé
couple
coupler
couplet
couplets
couplings
coupon
courage
courageous
courier
course
courser
court
courteous
courtesy

courthouse
courtier
courtliness
courtly
courtship
courtyard
cousin
cove
covenant
cover
coverage
coverlet
coverlets
covert
covet
covetous
coward
cowardice
cowardly
cowboy
cowcatcher
cowl
cowlick
coworker
coxcomb
coy
coyly
coyness
coyote
crab
crack

cracker
crackle
crackled
cradle
cradled
craft
craftier
craftiest
craftily
craftiness
craftsman
crafty
crag
cram
crammed
cramp
cranberry
crane
craned
cranial
craniotomy
cranium
crank
crankcase
cranked
crankily
crankiness
cranky
cranny
crape
crash

crass
crate
crated
crater
cravat
crave
craven
cravenette
cravings
crawfish
crawl
crawled
crayon
craze
crazier
craziest
crazily
craziness
crazy
creak
creakingly
cream
creamery
creamier
creamiest
creamy
crease
create
created
creation
creative

creator
creature
credence
credential
credibility
credible
credit
creditable
credited
creditor
credo
credulity
credulous
creed
creek
creep
creeper
creepiness
cremate
cremated
cremation
crematory
Cremona
creole
creosote
crepitant
crepitate
crescendo
crescent
crest
crestfallen

cretin
cretonne
crevasse
crevice
crew
crewel
crib
cribbage
cricket
crime
criminal
criminally
criminology
crimp
crimson
cringe
crinkle
crinoline
cripple
crises
crisis
crisp
crisply
crispness
crisscross
criteria
criterion
critic
critical
critically
criticism

criticize
criticized
critique
croak
croaker
croakingly
crochet
crock
crockery
crocodile
crocus
crook
crooked
croon
crooned
crooner
crop
croquet
croquette
crosier
cross
crossbar
crossbow
crosscut
crossings
crossroad
crosswise
crotchet
crouch
croup
crow

crowbar
crowd
crowded
crown
crowned
crucial
crucially
crucible
crucifixion
cruciform
crude
crudity
cruel
cruelly
cruelty
cruise
cruiser
crumb
crumble
crumpet
crumple
crumpled
crunch
crusade
crusader
cruse
crush
crushingly
crust
crusty
crutch

crux
cry
cryolite
crypt
cryptic
cryptical
cryptically
cryptogram
cryptograph
cryptography
crystal
crystalline
crystallization
crystallize
crystallized
cub
cube
cubeb
cubic
cubicle
cubit
cuckoo
cucumber
cuddle
cuddled
cudgel
cue
cuff
cuirass
cuisine
culinary

cull
culled
culminate
culminated
culmination
culpability
culpable
culprit
cult
cultivate
cultivated
cultivation
cultivator
cultural
culturally
culture
cultured
culvert
cumbersome
cumulative
cuneiform
cunningly
cupboard
cupel
cupellation
cupful
Cupid
cupidity
cupola
cur
curable

curacy
curare
curate
curative
curator
curb
curbed
curd
cure
cured
curette
curfew
curio
curiosities
curiosity
curious
curiously
curl
curled
curler
curlicue
curly
curmudgeon
currant
currency
current
currently
curricula
curriculum
curse
cursive

cursory	cute	cyclopedic
curt	cuticle	Cyclops
curtail	cutlass	cyclotron
curtain	cutlery	cygnet
curtly	cutlet	cylinder
curvature	cutlets	cylindric
curve	cutout	cylindrical
curved	cutter	cymbal
cushion	cuttings	cynic
cusp	cuttlefish	cynical
cuspidor	cyanate	cynically
custard	cyanic	cynicism
custodial	cyanide	cynosure
custodian	cyanite	cypress
custody	cyanogen	cyst
custom	cyanosis	cystitis
customarily	cycle	cystoid
customary	cyclometer	cystolith
customer	cyclone	cystotomy
cut	cyclonic	czar
cutaneous	cyclopedia	Czech

D

dachshund
dacoit
daedal
daffodil
daft
dagger
daguerreotype
dahlia
daily
daintier
daintiest
daintily
daintiness
dainty
dairy
dairyman
dais
daisy
dalliance
dally
dalmatian
dam
damage
damaged
damascene
damascus
damask

dammed
damnable
damp
dampen
dampened
damper
dampest
dampness
dance
dancer
dandelion
dandle
dandled
dandruff
dandy
danger
dangerous
dangerously
dangle
dangled
Danish
dank
dapper
dapple
dappled
dare
dared

daringly
dark
darken
darker
darkest
darkly
darkness
darling
dart
dash
dastardly
data
date
dated
dative
datum
daub
daughter
daughter-in-law
daunt
daunted
dauntless
dauphin
davenport
davit
dawdle
dawdled

dawn
dawned
day
daybook
daybreak
daydream
daylight
daytime
dazzle
dazzled
dazzlingly
deacon
dead
deaden
deadened
deadfall
deadhead
deadlock
deadly
deaf
deafen
deafened
deafeningly
deafer
deafest
deal
dealer
dealings
dean
deanery
dear

dearer
dearest
dearly
dearth
death
deathbed
deathblow
deathless
deathly
debacle
debar
debark
debarred
debase
debased
debasement
debatable
debate
debated
debater
debauch
debauchery
debenture
debilitate
debilitated
debility
debit
debited
debt
debtor
debut

decade
decadence
decadent
decalcomania
decant
decanter
decapitate
decapitation
decathlon
decay
decease
decedent
deceit
deceitful
deceive
deceived
deceleration
December
decency
decennial
decent
decently
decentralization
decentralize
deception
deceptive
deceptively
decide
decidedly
deciduous
decimal

decimate
decimation
decipher
decipherable
deciphered
decision
decisive
decisively
decisiveness
deck
deckle
declaim
declamation
declamatory
declaration
declarative
declaratory
declare
declared
declension
declination
decline
declined
declivity
decoction
decompose
decomposition
decontaminate
decontamination
decorate
decorated
decoration
decorative
decorator
decorous
decorously
decorum
decoy
decrease
decreased
decreasingly
decree
decrepitude
decretal
decried
decry
dedicate
dedicated
dedication
dedicatory
deduce
deduced
deducible
deduct
deductible
deduction
deductively
deed
deeded
deem
deemed
deep
deepen
deepened
deeper
deepest
deeply
deepness
deer
deerskin
deface
defacement
defalcate
defalcated
defalcation
defamation
defamatory
defame
defamed
default
defaulter
defeasible
defeat
defect
defection
defective
defend
defendant
defended
defender
defense
defensible
defensive

defensively
defer
deference
deferential
deferment
deferred
defiance
defiant
defiantly
deficiency
deficient
deficit
defilade
defile
defiled
defilement
define
defined
definite
definitely
definiteness
definition
definitive
definitively
deflate
deflated
deflect
deflected
deflection
deforestation
deform

deformation
deformed
deformity
defraud
defrauded
defray
defrayed
deft
deftly
defunct
defy
degeneracy
degenerate
degenerately
degeneration
degradation
degrade
degraded
degradingly
degree
dehydrate
dehydration
deification
deify
deign
deigned
deism
deist
deity
dejectedly
dejection

delay
delectable
delectation
delegate
delegated
delegation
delete
deleted
deleterious
deletion
delftware
deliberate
deliberation
deliberative
delicacy
delicate
delicately
delicatessen
delicious
deliciously
delight
delightful
delightfully
delimit
delimitation
delineate
delineated
delineation
delineator
delinquency
delinquent

deliquesce
deliquescence
deliquescent
delirious
delirium
deliver
deliverance
deliverer
delivery
delphinium
delta
delude
deluded
deluge
delusion
delusive
de luxe
delve
demagnetize
demagogue
demand
demandingly
demarcation
demean
demeanor
demented
dementia
demerit
demigod
demise
demobilization
demobilize
demobilized
democracy
democrat
democratic
democratically
democratize
demolish
demolished
demolition
demon
demonetization
demonetize
demonstrable
demonstrate
demonstration
demonstrative
demonstrator
demoralization
demoralize
demoralized
demotic
demountable
demur
demure
demurely
demurrage
demurred
demurrer
den
denature
denatured
denial
denied
denizen
denominate
denominated
denomination
denominational
denotation
denote
denoted
denounce
dense
density
dent
dental
dentalgia
dented
dentifrice
dentist
dentistry
dentition
denunciation
denunciatory
deny
deodorant
deodorize
deodorized
depart
department
departmental

departure
depend
depended
dependency
dependent
depict
depiction
depilatory
deplete
depleted
depletion
deplorable
deplore
deplored
deploy
deployment
depolarization
depolarize
depopulate
deport
deportation
deportment
depose
deposed
deposit
depositary
deposited
deposition
depositor
depository
depot

depravation
deprave
depravity
deprecate
deprecated
deprecation
deprecatingly
deprecatory
depreciate
depreciated
depreciation
depredation
depress
depressant
depressingly
depression
depressive
deprivation
deprive
depth
deputation
depute
deputed
deputize
deputy
derail
derailment
derange
deranged
derangement
derelict

dereliction
deride
derision
derisive
derivation
derivative
derive
dermal
dermatitis
dermatology
derogatory
derrick
dervish
descend
descendant
descent
describe
described
description
descriptive
descry
desecrate
desecrated
desecration
desensitize
desert
desertion
deserve
deserved
deservedly
desiccant

desiccate
desiccator
desiderata
desideratum
design
designate
designated
designation
designed
designer
desirability
desirable
desire
desires
desirous
desist
desists
desk
desolate
desolately
desolation
despair
despaired
despairingly
desperate
desperately
desperation
despicable
despise
despised
despite

despoil
despoiled
despondency
despondent
despot
despotic
despotism
desquamated
desquamation
dessert
destination
destine
destined
destiny
destitute
destitution
destroy
destroyer
destructible
destruction
destructive
desuetude
desultorily
desultory
detach
detachable
detached
detachment
detail
detailed
detain

detained
detect
detection
detective
detector
detention
deter
detergent
deteriorate
deterioration
determinable
determination
determinative
determine
determined
deterred
deterrent
detest
detestable
detestation
detests
dethrone
detonate
detonated
detonation
detonator
detour
detoured
detract
detraction
detractor

detriment
detrimental
detritus
devaluate
devaluated
devaluation
devastate
devastated
devastation
develop
development
developmental
deviate
deviated
deviation
device
devil
deviltry
devious
deviously
deviousness
devise
devised
devitalize
devoid
devolve
devolved
devote
devoted
devotee
devotion

devotional
devour
devoured
devoutly
dew
dewy
dexter
dexterity
dexterous
dexterously
dextrose
diabetes
diabetic
diabolic
diabolical
diaconal
diacritical
diadem
diaeresis
diagnose
diagnosed
diagnoses
diagnosis
diagnostic
diagnostician
diagonal
diagram
dial
dialect
dialed
dialogue

diameter
diametric
diamond
diapason
diaper
diaphanous
diaphanously
diaphragm
diastole
diastolic
diathermic
diatom
diatonic
diatribe
dice
dichotomy
dictaphone
dictate
dictated
dictation
dictator
dictatorial
dictatorially
dictatorship
diction
dictionary
dictograph
dictum
did
didactic
die

died
diet
dietary
dietetics
differ
differed
difference
different
differential
differentiate
differentiated
differentiation
difficult
difficulty
diffidence
diffident
diffract
diffraction
diffuse
diffused
diffusion
dig
digest
digestible
digestion
digestive
diggings
digit
digitalis
dignify
dignitary

dignity
digress
digression
dike
dilapidate
dilapidation
dilatation
dilate
dilation
dilatory
dilemma
diligence
diligent
diligently
dilute
diluted
dilution
dim
dime
dimension
dimensional
diminish
diminuendo
diminution
diminutive
dimity
dimly
dimmed
dimmer
dimmest
dimness

dine
dined
diner
dingily
dingy
dinner
dinosaur
dint
diocese
diopter
diorama
diphtheria
diphthong
diploma
diplomacy
diplomat
diplomatic
diplomatist
diplopia
dipper
dipsomania
dipsomaniac
direct
direction
directive
directly
directness
director
directorate
directory
direful

direest
dirge
dirigible
dirndl
dirt
dirtily
dirty
disability
disable
disabuse
disadvantage
disadvantageous
disaffected
disaffection
disaffirm
disaffirmed
disagree
disagreeable
disagreement
disallow
disappear
disappearance
disappoint
disappointingly
disappointment
disapprobation
disapproval
disarm
disarmament
disarmed
disarmingly

disarrange
disarray
disarticulate
disassociate
disaster
disastrous
disastrously
disavow
disavowal
disband
disbanded
disbar
disbarment
disbarred
disbelieve
disbeliever
disbelievingly
disburse
disbursement
discard
discarded
discern
discerned
discernible
discerningly
discernment
discharge
discharged
disciple
discipleship
disciplinary

discipline
disciplined
disclaim
disclaimed
disclaimer
disclose
disclosure
discolor
discoloration
discomfit
discomfiture
discomfort
discommode
discompose
discomposure
disconcert
disconnect
disconnected
disconsolate
disconsolately
discontent
discontented
discontentment
discontinuance
discontinue
discontinued
discord
discordant
discount
discountenance
discourage

discouraged
discouragement
discouragingly
discourse
discourteous
discourtesy
discover
discoverer
discovery
discredit
discreditable
discredited
discreet
discrepancy
discrete
discretion
discretionary
discriminate
discriminated
discrimination
discriminative
discriminatory
discursive
discus
discuss
discusses
discussion
disdain
disdained
disdainful
disease

diseased
disembarkation
disembarrass
disembody
disenchant
disengage
disesteem
disfavor
disfeature
disfigure
disfigured
disfigurement
disgorge
disgrace
disgraced
disgraceful
disgruntle
disguise
disguised
disgust
disgustedly
disgustingly
dish
dishabille
disharmony
dishearten
dishevel
dishonest
dishonestly
dishonor
dishonorable

dishonored
disillusion
disinclination
disincline
disinclined
disinfect
disinfectant
disingenuous
disinherit
disintegrate
disinterested
disinterestedly
disjoin
disjoined
disjoinings
disjunction
disjunctive
disk
dislike
dislocate
dislocated
dislocation
dislodge
disloyal
disloyalty
dismal
dismally
dismantle
dismantled
dismast
dismasted

dismay
dismayed
dismember
dismembered
dismemberment
dismiss
dismissal
dismount
dismounted
disobedience
disobedient
disobey
disobeyed
disoblige
disorder
disorderly
disorganize
disown
disparage
disparagement
disparagingly
disparate
disparity
dispassionate
dispatch
dispatched
dispatcher
dispel
dispelled
dispensable
dispensary

dispensation
dispense
dispensed
dispersal
disperse
dispersed
dispersion
dispirited
displace
displacement
display
displease
displeasure
disport
disposal
dispose
disposed
disposition
dispossess
dispossessed
disposure
dispraise
disproof
disproportion
disproportionate
disputable
disputant
disputation
disputatious
dispute
disputed

disqualification
disqualify
disquiet
disquietude
disquisition
disregard
disrepair
disreputable
disrepute
disrespect
disrespectful
disrobe
disroot
disrupt
disruption
disruptive
dissatisfaction
dissatisfy
dissect
dissemble
disseminate
disseminated
dissemination
dissension
dissent
dissenter
dissentient
dissertation
disservice
dissidence
dissident

dissimilar
dissimilarity
dissimulate
dissimulated
dissimulation
dissipate
dissipated
dissipation
dissociate
dissociated
dissociation
dissolute
dissolution
dissolve
dissolved
dissonance
dissonant
dissuade
dissuasion
distaff
distal
distance
distant
distaste
distasteful
distemper
distend
distensible
distill
distillate
distillation

distilled
distiller
distillery
distinct
distinction
distinctive
distinctively
distinctly
distinctness
distinguish
distort
distorted
distortion
distract
distractingly
distraction
distrain
distrained
distraught
distress
distressingly
distribute
distribution
distributive
distributor
district
distrust
distrustful
disturb
disturbance
disturbed

disturber
disunion
disunite
disuse
ditto
ditty
diurnal
divagate
divan
dive
dived
diver
diverge
diverged
divergence
divergent
diverse
diversification
diversify
diversion
diversionary
diversity
divert
divest
divide
divided
dividend
divider
divination
divine
divined

divinely
divinity
divisibility
divisible
division
divisor
divorce
divorcee
divorcement
divulge
divulged
dizzier
dizziest
dizzily
dizziness
dizzy
do
docile
docility
dock
docket
doctor
doctorate
doctrinaire
doctrinal
doctrine
document
documentary
documentation
dodder
dodge
dodged
dodo
doe
doeskin
doff
dog
dogcart
doge
dogged
doggerel
dogma
dogmatic
dogmatism
dogmatize
dogtrot
dogwood
doily
doings
doldrums
dole
doled
doleful
doll
dollar
dolman
dolphin
dolt
domain
dome
domed
domestic
domesticate
domesticated
domesticity
domicile
domiciliary
dominance
dominant
dominate
dominated
domination
domineer
domineered
domineeringly
dominie
dominion
domino
donate
donated
donation
donative
donkey
donor
doom
doomed
door
doorknob
doorsill
doorway
dope
dormant
dormer

dormitory
dormouse
dorsal
dory
dosage
dose
dot
dotage
dotard
dote
dotingly
dotted
double
doubly
doubt
doubted
doubter
doubtful
doubtfully
doubtingly
doubtless
dough
doughboy
doughnut
doughty
doughy
dour
dove
dove
dovecote
dovetail

dowager
dowdier
dowdiest
dowdily
dowdy
dowel
doweled
down
downcast
downfall
downhearted
downhill
downpour
downright
downstairs
downward
downy
dowry
doxology
doze
dozen
drab
draft
draftier
draftiest
draftily
drafty
drag
draggle
draggled
dragnet

dragon
dragoon
dragooned
drain
drainage
drained
drainer
drainpipe
drake
dram
drama
dramatic
dramatics
dramatist
dramatization
dramatize
dramaturgy
drape
draper
drapery
drastic
draw
drawback
drawbar
drawbridge
drawee
drawer
drawings
drawl
drawn
drawplate

dray
drayage
drayman
dread
dreaded
dreadful
dream
dreamed
dreamier
dreamiest
dreamily
dreamless
dreamlike
dreamy
drearily
dreariness
dreary
dredge
dredged
dreg
drench
drenched
dress
dressed
dresser
dressings
dressmaker
dressy
drew
dribble
dribbled

dried
drier
driest
drift
driftwood
drill
drilled
drink
drinkable
drinker
drip
drippings
drive
drivel
driven
driver
driveway
drizzle
drizzled
droll
drollery
dromedary
drone
droningly
drool
droolings
droop
drop
dropper
droppings
dropsical

dropsy
dross
drought
drove
drown
drowned
drownings
drowse
drowsily
drowsiness
drowsy
drudge
drudgery
drug
druggist
druid
drum
drumhead
drummed
drunk
drunkard
drunken
dry
dryly
dual
duality
dubiety
dubious
ducal
ducat
duchess

duck
duckling
duckpin
duckweed
duct
ductile
ductility
dudgeon
due
duel
duelist
duenna
duffer
dug
dugong
dugout
duke
dukedom
dulcet
dulcimer
dull
dullard
duller
dullest
dullness

dully
dumb
dummy
dump
dumpling
dun
dunce
dune
dungaree
dungeon
dunnage
dunned
dupe
duplex
duplicate
duplication
duplicator
duplicity
durability
durable
durance
duration
duress
during
dusky

dust
dusted
duster
dustiness
dusty
duteous
duties
dutiful
duty
dwarf
dwarfish
dwell
dwellings
dwelt
dwindle
dwindled
dynamic
dynamism
dynamite
dynamo
dynasty
dynatron
dysfunction
dyspepsia
dyspeptic

E

each
eager
eagerly
eagerness
eagle
eaglet
ear
earl
earldom
earlier
earliest
early
earmark
earn
earned
earnest
earnestly
earring
earshot
earthen
earthenware
earthly
earthquake
earthward
earthwork
earthworm
ease

eased
easel
easement
easier
easiest
easily
east
Easter
easterly
eastern
easterner
eastward
eastwardly
easy
eat
eatable
eater
eavesdrop
ebb
ebonize
ebony
ebullience
ebullient
ebullition
eccentric
eccentricity
ecchymosis

ecclesiastic
ecclesiastical
echelon
echo
éclair
éclat
eclectic
eclecticism
eclipse
eclogue
economic
economical
economically
economize
economized
economy
ecru
ecstasy
ecstatic
ecstatically
eczema
eddy
edelweiss
edge
edged
edgeways
edgewise

edgings
edibility
edible
edict
edification
edifice
edify
edit
edited
edition
editor
editorial
editorially
educable
educate
education
educational
educationally
educator
eel
efface
effacement
effect
effected
effective
effectual
effectually
effectuate
effeminacy
effeminate
effervesce
effervescence
effervescent
effete
efficacious
efficacy
efficiency
efficient
effigies
effigy
efflorescence
efflorescent
effluvia
effluvium
effort
effortless
effrontery
effulgence
effulgent
effusion
effusive
effusively
effusiveness
eggnog
eggplant
eggshell
ego
egoism
egoist
egotistic
egotistical
egregious
egress
Egyptian
eider
either
ejaculate
ejaculation
eject
ejection
ejectment
ejector
elaborate
elaborately
elaboration
elapse
elastic
elasticity
elated
elation
elbow
elbowed
elbowroom
elder
elderberry
elderly
eldest
elect
election
electioneer
elective
elector
electoral

electorate
electrical
electrically
electrician
electricity
electrification
electrify
electrocute
electrocution
electrode
electrolier
electrolysis
electrolytic
electrolytical
electrolyze
electromagnet
electrometer
electron
electronic
electroplate
electropositive
electroscope
electrotype
eleemosynary
elegance
elegant
elegy
element
elemental
elementally
elementary

elephant
elephantiasis
elephantine
elevate
elevation
elevator
elfin
elicit
elide
eligibility
eligible
eliminate
eliminated
elimination
eliminative
elision
elite
elixir
Elizabethan
elk
ellipsis
ellipsoid
elliptic
elliptical
elm
elocution
elocutionist
elongate
elongated
elongation
elope

elopement
eloquence
eloquent
eloquently
else
elsewhere
elucidate
elucidated
elucidation
elude
eluded
elusive
emaciate
emaciated
emaciation
emanate
emanated
emanation
emancipate
emancipated
emancipation
emancipator
emasculate
emasculation
embalm
embalmer
embankment
embargo
embarkation
embarrass
embarrassed

embarrassment
embassy
embattle
embattled
embellish
embellishment
ember
embezzle
embezzled
embezzlement
embezzler
embitter
embittered
emblazon
emblem
emblematic
emblematical
embodiment
embody
embolden
emboldened
embolism
embolus
emboss
embrace
embrasure
embrocation
embroider
embroidered
embroidery
embroil

embryo
embryonic
emend
emendation
emerald
emerge
emergence
emergency
emergent
emeritus
emery
emetic
emigrant
emigrate
emigration
eminence
eminent
emissary
emission
emit
emitted
emollient
emolument
emotion
emotional
emotionally
emperor
emphases
emphasis
emphasize
emphasized

emphatic
empire
empiric
empirical
empiricism
emplacement
employ
employee
employer
employment
emporium
empower
empowered
empress
emptied
emptily
emptiness
empty
empyema
emu
emulate
emulated
emulates
emulation
emulative
emulatory
emulous
emulsification
emulsify
emulsion
enable

enact
enacted
enactment
enamel
enameled
enamored
encamp
encampment
encaustic
encephalic
encephalitis
enchant
enchanted
enchantingly
enchantment
encircle
encircled
encirclement
enclave
enclose
enclosure
encomia
encomium
encompass
encore
encounter
encountered
encourage
encouraged
encouragement
encouragingly

encroach
encroachment
encumber
encumbered
encumbrance
encyclical
encyclopedia
encyclopedic
encysted
end
endanger
endangered
endear
endeared
endeavor
endeavored
ended
endemic
endings
endive
endless
endlessly
endlong
endocrine
endocrinology
endoderm
endogenous
endorse
endorsement
endow
endowed

endowment
endue
endurable
endurance
endure
endured
enduringly
endways
endwise
enemy
energetic
energies
energize
energized
energy
enervate
enervation
enfeeble
enfilade
enfold
enforce
enforceable
enforcement
enforcer
enfranchise
engage
engaged
engagement
engagingly
engender
engendered

engine
engineer
English
Englishman
engorge
engorgement
engrain
engrained
engrave
engraved
engraver
engross
engrossed
engrosser
engulf
enhance
enhancement
enharmonic
enigma
enigmatic
enigmatical
enjoin
enjoined
enjoy
enjoyable
enjoyment
enlarge
enlarged
enlargement
enlarger
enlighten
enlightened
enlightenment
enlist
enlisted
enlistment
enliven
enlivened
enmesh
enmity
ennoble
enormity
enormous
enough
enrage
enrapture
enraptured
enrich
enrichment
enroll
enrolled
enrollment
enshrine
ensign
ensilage
enslave
enslavement
ensue
ensure
entablature
entail
entailed
entangle
entanglement
enter
enteralgia
enterectomy
entered
enteritis
enterotomy
enterprise
entertain
entertained
entertainer
entertainingly
entertainment
enthrall
enthrone
enthusiasm
enthusiast
enthusiastic
enthusiastically
entice
enticed
enticement
enticingly
entire
entirety
entitle
entitled
entity
entomb
entombed

entombment
entomologist
entomology
entrails
entrance
entrancingly
entrant
entrap
entreat
entreaty
entrust
entrusted
entry
entryway
entwine
enucleate
enucleation
enumerate
enumeration
enumerator
enunciate
enunciation
enunciator
envelope
enviable
envious
environment
environmental
environs
envisage
envoy

envoys
envy
enzyme
eon
ephemeral
epic
epicure
epicurean
epidemic
epidermal
epidermic
epidermis
epidermoid
epiglottis
epigram
epigraph
epilepsy
epileptic
epileptoid
epilogue
episcopal
episcopalian
episode
episodic
epistemology
epistle
epitaph
epithalamium
epithet
epitome
epitomize

epizootic
epoch
equable
equably
equal
equaled
equality
equalization
equalize
equalized
equalizer
equally
equanimity
equate
equation
equator
equatorial
equerry
equestrian
equiangular
equidistance
equidistant
equilateral
equilibrium
equine
equinoctial
equinox
equip
equipage
equipment
equipoise

equitable
equitation
equity
equivalent
equivocal
equivocate
equivocation
era
eradicate
eradication
erase
erased
eraser
erasure
erect
erectile
erection
erectness
erg
ergo
ergot
ermine
erode
erosion
err
errand
errata
erratic
erratically
erratum
erred

erroneous
error
eructation
erudite
erudition
erupt
eruption
eruptive
erysipelas
escalade
escalator
escapade
escape
escapement
escarpment
escheat
eschew
escort
escorted
escritoire
escrow
escutcheon
Eskimo
esophagus
esoteric
esparto
especial
especially
Esperanto
espionage
esplanade

espousal
espouse
esprit
espy
esquire
essay
essayist
essence
essential
essentially
establish
establishment
estate
esteem
esteemed
ester
esthetic
estimable
estimate
estimated
estimation
estimator
estivate
estoppel
estrange
estranged
estrangement
estron
estuary
esurient
etch

etcher
etchings
eternal
eternally
eternity
ethane
ether
ethereal
ethereally
ethical
ethically
ethics
ethnology
ethyl
etiquette
etymological
etymology
eucalyptus
Eucharist
euchre
Euclid
eugenics
eulogistic
eulogize
eulogy
euphemism
euphemistic
euphonious
euphony
Eurasian
eureka

European
Eustachian
eutectic
evacuate
evacuated
evacuation
evade
evaded
evaluate
evaluation
evanescence
evanescent
evangelical
evangelist
evaporate
evaporation
evaporator
evasion
evasive
evasively
evasiveness
even
evening
evenings
evenly
evenness
event
eventful
eventfully
eventual
eventualities

eventuality
eventually
eventuate
ever
everglade
evergreen
everlasting
everlastingly
every
everybody
everyday
everyone
everything
everywhere
evict
evicted
eviction
evidence
evident
evidently
evidential
evil
evilly
evince
eviscerate
evocation
evocative
evoke
evolution
evolutionary
evolutionist

evolve
ewe
ewer
exacerbate
exacerbation
exact
exaction
exactitude
exactly
exactness
exaggerate
exaggerated
exaggeration
exalt
exaltation
exalted
examinable
examination
examine
examined
examiner
example
exasperate
exasperatingly
exasperation
excavate
excavation
excavator
exceed
exceeded
exceedingly

excel
excelled
excellence
excellency
excellent
excelsior
except
exception
exceptional
exceptionally
excerpt
excess
excesses
excessive
excessively
exchange
exchequer
excipient
excise
excision
excitability
excitable
excitant
excitation
excite
excitedly
excitement
exclaim
exclaimed
exclamation
exclamatory

exclosure
exclude
excluded
exclusion
exclusive
excommunicate
excommunication
excoriate
excoriated
excoriation
excrescence
excrete
excretion
excretory
excruciate
excruciated
excruciatingly
excruciation
exculpate
exculpated
exculpation
exculpatory
excursion
excusable
excuse
excused
excuses
execrable
execrate
execration
executant

execute
executed
execution
executioner
executive
executor
executrix
exegeses
exegesis
exemplar
exemplary
exemplification
exemplify
exempt
exempted
exemption
exequatur
exercise
exercised
exerciser
exert
exerted
exertion
exhalation
exhale
exhaled
exhaust
exhaustion
exhaustive
exhaustively
exhaustless

exhibit
exhibited
exhibition
exhibitor
exhilarate
exhilaration
exhort
exhortation
exhorted
exhumation
exhume
exigency
exigent
exiguous
exile
exist
existence
existent
exists
exit
exodus
exonerate
exoneration
exorbitant
exorbitantly
exorcise
exorcised
exorcism
exordium
exoteric
exotic

expand
expanded
expanse
expansion
expansive
expatiate
expatiated
expatriate
expatriation
expect
expectancy
expectant
expectantly
expectation
expectorant
expectorate
expectoration
expediency
expedient
expediently
expeditate
expedite
expedited
expedition
expeditionary
expeditious
expeditiously
expel
expelled
expend
expended

expenditure
expense
expensively
experience
experienced
experiences
experiment
experimental
experimentally
experimentation
experimenter
expert
expertly
expertness
expiate
expiation
expiration
expire
expired
explain
explained
explanation
explanatory
expletive
explicable
explicit
explicitly
explode
exploded
exploit
exploitation

exploited
exploration
exploratory
explore
explored
explorer
exploringly
explosion
explosive
exponent
exponential
export
exportable
exportation
expose
exposed
exposition
expositor
expository
expostulate
expostulated
expostulation
exposure
expound
express
expressage
expression
expressive
expressively
expressly
expressman

expropriate
expropriation
expulsion
expunge
expunged
expurgate
expurgated
expurgation
exquisite
extant
extemporaneous
extempore
extemporization
extemporize
extend
extended
extensible
extension
extensive
extent
extenuate
extenuated
extenuation
exterior
exterminate
exterminated
extermination
exterminator
external
externally
extinct

extinction
extinguish
extirpate
extirpated
extirpation
extol
extort
extorted
extortion
extortionate
extra
extract
extraction
extractive
extradite
extradited
extradition
extraneous
extraordinarily

extraordinary
extravagance
extravagant
extravaganza
extravasate
extravasation
extreme
extremist
extremity
extricate
extricated
extrication
extrinsic
extrude
extruded
extrusion
exuberance
exuberant
exudate

exudation
exude
exult
exultant
exultation
exulted
exultingly
eye
eyeball
eyebrow
eyelash
eyeless
eyelet
eyelid
eyepiece
eyes
eyeshot
eyesight
eyespot

F

Fabian
fable
fabric
fabricate
fabrication
fabulous
façade
face
facet
facetious
facial
facile
facilely
facilitate
facilities
facility
facings
facsimile
fact
faction
factional
factious
factitious
factitive
factor
factory
factotum
factual
factually
facultative
faculties
faculty
faddist
fade
faded
Fahrenheit
fail
failed
failings
faille
failure
faint
fainted
fainthearted
faintly
faintness
fair
fairer
fairest
fairly
fairness
fairway
fairy
fairyland
faith
faithful
faithfulness
faithless
faithlessly
fake
faker
falcon
fall
fallacious
fallaciously
fallacy
fallen
fallibility
fallible
fallow
false
falsehood
falsely
falseness
falsetto
falsification
falsifier
falsify
falsity
falter
faltered

falteringly
fame
famed
familial
familiar
familiarity
familiarize
familiarly
families
family
famine
famish
famous
famously
fan
fanatic
fanatical
fanaticism
fancied
fancier
fanciest
fanciful
fancy
fanfare
fang
fanged
fanlight
fanned
fantasia
fantastic
fantasy

far
farad
farce
farcical
farcy
fare
fared
farewell
farina
farinaceous
farm
farmed
farmhouse
farmyard
faro
farsighted
farther
farthest
farthing
fascinate
fascinatingly
fashion
fashionable
fast
fasten
fastened
fastenings
faster
fastest
fastidious
fastness

fat
fatal
fatalism
fatalist
fatalistic
fatality
fatally
fate
fateful
father
fatherhood
father-in-law
fatherland
fatherless
fatherly
fathom
fathomless
fatigue
fatness
fatten
fatter
fattest
fatty
fatuity
fatuous
faucet
fault
faultily
faultless
faultlessly
faulty

faun
fauna
favor
favorable
favored
favorite
favoritism
fawn
fawned
fealty
fear
feared
fearful
fearless
fearlessly
fearsome
feasibility
feasible
feast
feat
feather
featherweight
feathery
feature
featured
febrile
February
fecund
fecundate
fecundity
federal
federalist
federalization
federalize
federalized
federate
federated
federation
federative
fedora
fee
feeble
feebleness
feeblest
feebly
feed
feedback
feedings
feel
feeler
feelingly
feelings
feet
feign
feigned
feint
feldspar
felicitate
felicitated
felicitation
felicitous
felicitously
felicity
feline
fellow
fellowship
felly
felon
felonious
felony
felt
felucca
female
feminine
femininely
femininity
feminist
femoral
femur
fen
fence
fencer
fend
fender
fenestrated
fenestration
Fenian
fennel
feral
ferment
fermentation
fermented
fern

ferocious
ferociously
ferocity
ferret
ferreted
ferric
ferrochrome
ferrotype
ferrule
ferry
ferryboat
fertile
fertility
fertilization
fertilize
fertilized
ferule
fervent
fervently
fervid
fervidly
fervor
fescue
festal
fester
festered
festival
festive
festivity
festoon
festooned

festoonery
fetch
fetid
fetish
fetishism
fetlock
fetter
fettered
fettle
feud
feudal
feudalism
feudatory
fever
feverish
feverishly
few
fez
fiasco
fiat
fib
fiber
fibroid
fibula
fickle
fiction
fictional
fictitious
fiddle
fiddler
fidelity

fidget
fiduciary
fief
field
fielded
fieldpiece
fiend
fiendish
fiendishly
fierce
fierceness
fiercer
fiercest
fiery
fife
fig
fight
figuration
figurative
figuratively
figure
figured
figurehead
figurine
filament
filariasis
filature
filbert
file
filed
filial

filibuster
filigree
filings
fill
filled
filler
fillet
film
filmed
filmy
filter
filtered
filth
filthier
filthiest
filthiness
filthy
filtrate
filtration
fin
final
finalist
finality
finally
finance
financial
financially
financier
finch
find
finder
findings
fine
fined
finely
fineness
finer
finery
finespun
finesse
finest
finger
fingered
fingerling
fingerprint
finial
finis
finish
finished
finisher
finite
fiord
fir
fire
firearm
firebrand
firebrick
fired
firefly
fireman
fireplace
fireproof
fireside
fireworks
firkin
firm
firmament
firmer
firmest
firmly
firmness
first
firstly
firth
fiscal
fish
fisherman
fishery
fishhook
fishline
fishwife
fishy
fissile
fission
fissionable
fissure
fist
fistic
fisticuffs
fistula
fit
fitful
fitfully

fitness
fitter
fittingly
fittings
fix
fixation
fixative
fixed
fixings
fixity
fixture
fizzle
fizzled
flabbier
flabbiest
flabbiness
flabby
flaccid
flag
flagellant
flagellate
flagellation
flageolet
flageolets
flagitious
flagon
flagpole
flagrance
flagrant
flagrantly
flagship
flagstaff
flagstone
flail
flailed
flair
flake
flakiness
flaky
flambeau
flamboyant
flame
flamed
flamingly
flamingo
flange
flanged
flank
flanked
flannel
flannelette
flap
flapjack
flare
flared
flash
flashboard
flasher
flashily
flashiness
flashingly
flashy
flask
flat
flatboat
flatfish
flatiron
flatly
flatness
flatten
flatter
flattered
flatterer
flatteringly
flattery
flattest
flatulence
flatulent
flatware
flatwise
flatworm
flaunt
flaunted
flauntingly
flautist
flavor
flavored
flavorings
flaw
flax
flaxen
flay
flea

fleabite
fleck
fledge
fledgling
flee
fleece
fleeced
fleeciness
fleecy
fleet
fleetingly
Flemish
flesh
fleshings
fleshy
Fletcherism
flew
flex
flexibility
flexible
flexure
flick
flicker
flickeringly
flier
flight
flightiness
flighty
flimsier
flimsiest
flimsily
flimsiness
flimsy
flinch
flinchingly
fling
flint
flintiness
flintlock
flinty
flippancy
flippant
flippantly
flipper
flirt
flirtation
flirtatious
flirted
flit
flitch
flivver
float
floated
floater
flocculence
flocculent
flock
floe
flog
floggings
flood
flooded
floodlight
floor
floppiness
floppy
floral
Florentine
floriculture
florid
floridly
florin
florist
floss
flossy
flotation
flotilla
flotsam
flounce
flounder
floundered
flounderingly
flour
flourish
flourishingly
floury
flout
flouted
flow
flower
flowered
floweriness
flowerpot

flowery
flowingly
flown
fluctuate
fluctuated
fluctuation
flue
fluency
fluent
fluently
fluff
fluffiness
fluffy
fluid
fluidity
fluidly
fluke
flume
flung
flunk
flunked
flunky
fluorescence
fluorescent
fluorine
fluoroscope
flurry
flush
fluster
flustered
fluted

flutings
flutist
flutter
fluttered
flutteringly
fluttery
flux
fluxion
fly
flyer
flyleaf
flytrap
flywheel
foal
foaled
foam
foamed
foamier
foamiest
foaminess
foamy
fob
focal
focalize
focus
fodder
foe
foeman
fog
foggy
foghorn

foible
foil
foiled
foist
fold
folded
folder
foliage
foliate
foliation
folio
folk
folkway
follicle
follicular
follow
followed
follower
folly
foment
fomentation
fomented
fond
fondant
fonder
fondest
fondle
fondled
fondly
fondness
fondue

font
food
fool
fooled
foolhardy
foolish
foolishly
foolishness
foolproof
foolscap
foot
footage
football
footboard
footbridge
footed
footfall
footgear
foothill
foothold
footings
footless
footlights
footman
footmark
footnote
footpace
footpad
footpath
footprint
footrest

footstep
footstool
footwear
foozle
foozled
foppery
for
forage
forasmuch
foray
forbear
forbearance
forbid
forbidden
forbiddingly
forebore
force
forceful
forcemeat
forceps
forces
forcible
ford
forded
forearm
forebear
forebode
forebodings
forecast
forecastle
foreclose

foreclosed
foreclosure
foredeck
foredoom
foredoomed
forefather
forefinger
forefoot
forefront
foregone
foreground
forehanded
forehead
foreign
foreigner
foreknowledge
foreleg
forelock
foreman
foremast
foremost
forename
forenoon
forensic
foreordain
foreordained
forequarter
forerunner
foresee
foreshadow
foreshore

foresight
forest
forestall
forestalled
forestation
forested
forester
forestry
forests
foretaste
foretell
forethought
foretold
forever
forewoman
foreword
forfeit
forfeiture
forgather
forgave
forge
forgery
forget
forgetful
forgetfully
forgetfulness
forgivable
forgive
forgiven
forgiveness
forgivingly

forgo
forgot
forgotten
fork
forked
forlorn
form
formal
formaldehyde
formalism
formality
formalize
formally
format
formation
formative
formed
former
formerly
formic
formidable
formula
formulate
formulated
formulates
formulation
forsake
forsaken
forsook
forsooth
forswear

forsythia
fort
fortalice
forth
forthcoming
forthright
forthrightness
forthwith
fortification
fortify
fortitude
fortnight
fortnightly
fortress
fortuitous
fortunate
fortune
forum
forward
forwarded
forwarder
forwardness
fossil
fossiliferous
fossilization
fossilize
fossilized
foster
fostered
fought
foul

foulard
fouler
foulest
foully
foulness
found
foundation
founded
founder
foundling
foundry
fount
fountain
fountainhead
foursome
fowl
fox
foxglove
foxier
foxiest
foxy
fracas
fraction
fractional
fractionally
fractionate
fractionation
fracture
fractured
fragile
fragilely
fragility
fragment
fragmentary
fragmentation
fragrance
fragrant
fragrantly
frail
frailty
frame
framed
framework
franc
franchise
frank
frankfurter
frankly
frankness
frantic
fraternal
fraternally
fraternity
fraternization
fraternize
fraternized
fratricide
fraud
fraudulent
fraught
fray
frazzle
frazzled
freak
freakish
freckle
freckled
free
freeboard
freeborn
freedom
freehand
freely
freeman
Freemason
Freemasonry
freestone
freeze
freezer
freight
freighter
French
frenzied
frenzy
frequency
frequent
frequently
fresco
fresh
freshen
freshened
freshly
freshman

fret
fretful
fretwork
friability
friable
friar
fricassee
friction
frictional
Friday
fried
friend
friendless
friendlier
friendliest
friendliness
friendly
friendship
frieze
frigate
fright
frighten
frightened
frighteningly
frightful
frightfully
frightfulness
frigid
frigidity
frigidly
frill

fringe
frippery
frisky
fritter
frittered
frivolity
frivolous
frivolously
frizzle
frizzled
frock
frog
frogfish
frolic
from
frond
fronded
front
frontage
frontal
fronted
frontier
frontispiece
frost
frostbite
frosted
frostfish
frostily
frostiness
frostwork
frosty

froth
frothed
frothy
froward
frown
frowned
frowningly
frowzily
frowzy
froze
frozen
fructiferous
frugal
frugality
frugally
fruit
fruiterer
fruitful
fruitfully
fruitfulness
fruition
fruitless
fruitlessly
fruitlessness
fruity
frump
frustrate
frustration
fry
fryer
fuchsia

fuddle
fuddled
fudge
fuel
fueled
fugacious
fugitive
fugue
fulcrum
fulfill
fulfillment
full
fuller
fullest
fully
fulminant
fulminate
fulminated
fulmination
fulsome
fumble
fumblingly
fume
fumed
fumigate
fumigated
fumigation
fumigator
fun
function
functional

functionary
fund
fundamental
fundamentally
funded
funeral
funereal
funereally
fungi
fungible
fungicide
fungoid
fungus
funicular
funnel
funnier
funniest
funny
fur
furbelow
furbish
furious
furiously
furl
furled
furlong
furlough
furloughed
furnace
furnish
furnished

furnishings
furniture
furor
furrier
furriest
furrow
furrowed
furry
further
furtherance
furthermore
furthermost
furthest
furtive
furtively
fury
fuse
fused
fuselage
fuses
fusibility
fusible
fusilade
fusion
fuss
fussy
futile
futilely
futility
future
futurity

G

gabardine
gable
gadfly
gadolinium
gadroon
gaff
gag
gage
gaiety
gaily
gain
gained
gainer
gainful
gainfully
gainsay
gaiter
galantine
galaxy
gale
galena
gall
gallant
gallantry
gallery
galley
gallium

gallon
gallop
gallows
gallstone
galvanism
galvanization
galvanize
galvanized
gambit
gambler
gamboge
gambol
gambrel
game
gameness
gammon
gamut
gander
gang
ganglia
ganglion
gangplank
gangrene
gangrenous
gangster
gangway
gap

garage
garb
garbage
garble
garden
gardener
gardenia
garish
garland
garlic
garment
garner
garnet
garnish
garnishee
garnisher
garnishment
garniture
garret
garrison
garrulity
garrulous
garter
gas
gaseous
gash
gasket

gasoline
gasp
gastralgia
gastric
gastritis
gastronomic
gate
gatehouse
gatekeeper
gatepost
gateway
gather
gatherer
gatherings
gaucherie
gaudy
gauge
gauntlet
gauntlets
gauze
gave
gavel
gavotte
gay
gayety
gayly
gayness
gaze
gazelle
gazette
gazetteer

gear
geared
geisha
gelatin
gelatinize
gelatinoid
gelatinous
gem
gemmed
gender
genealogical
genealogist
genealogy
genera
general
generalissimo
generality
generalization
generalize
generalized
generally
generalship
generate
generation
generative
generator
generic
generosity
generous
generously
genesis

genetics
genial
geniality
genially
genii
genitive
genius
geniuses
genteel
gentian
gentile
gentility
gentle
gentleman
gentlemen
gentleness
gentler
gentlest
gently
gentry
genuflect
genuflection
genuine
genuinely
genuineness
genus
geodetic
geography
geological
geology
geometric

geometry
geranium
gerent
germ
German
germane
germicide
germinal
germinant
germinate
germinated
germination
germinative
gerund
gerundial
gerundive
gesso
Gestalt
gesticulate
gesture
gestured
get
geyser
ghastliness
ghastly
gherkin
ghetto
ghost
ghostliness
ghostly
ghoul

giant
gibber
gibbered
gibberish
gibbon
gibe
giblets
giddiness
giddy
gift
gifted
gig
gigantic
giggle
giggled
gild
gilded
gilder
gill
gill
gilt
gimbals
gimlet
gimlets
gin
ginger
gingerly
gingham
gingivitis
giraffe
gird

girded
girder
girdle
girdled
girl
girlhood
girlish
girth
give
given
giver
gizzard
glacial
glad
gladden
gladdened
glade
gladiator
gladiatorial
gladiolus
gladly
gladness
Gladstone
glamorous
glamour
glance
glanced
gland
glandered
glanders
glandular

glare
glared
glaringly
glass
glassful
glasshouse
glassiness
glassware
glassy
glaze
glazed
glazier
gleam
gleamed
glean
gleaner
gleeful
glib
glibly
glide
glided
glider
glidingly
glimmer
glimpse
glint
glioma
glissando
glisten
glistened
glitter

glittered
global
globe
globular
globule
gloom
gloomily
gloominess
gloria
glorification
glorify
glorious
glory
gloss
glossal
glossary
glossily
glossiness
glossitis
glossy
glottis
glove
glover
glow
glower
glowered
glowingly
glowworm
glucinum
glucose
glue

glued
glum
glut
glutted
glutton
gluttonous
gluttonously
gluttony
glycerin
gnarl
gnarled
gnash
gnat
gnathic
gnaw
gnawed
gneiss
gnome
gnomic
gnomon
gnu
go
goal
goat
goatfish
goatherd
gobble
goblet
goblets
goblin
gocart

god
godchild
goddess
godfather
godhead
godhood
godless
godlike
godliness
godly
godparent
godsend
godson
goggle
goings
goiter
gold
golden
goldenrod
goldfinch
goldfish
goldsmith
golf
golfer
gondola
gondolier
gone
gong
goober
good
good-by

goodly
good-natured
goodness
goose
gooseberry
gopher
Gordian
gore
gored
gorge
gorgeous
gorget
gorilla
gospel
gossamer
gossip
got
Gothic
gotten
gouache
gouge
gouged
goulash
gourd
gourmet
gout
govern
governable
governance
governess
government

governmental
governor
gown
grab
grace
graceful
graceless
gracious
graciously
grackle
gradation
grade
graded
gradient
gradual
gradually
graduate
graduated
graduation
graft
grafted
grafter
grail
grain
grained
grammar
grammarian
grammatical
granary
grand
grandchild

grandee
grandeur
grandfather
grandiloquence
grandiloquent
grandiose
grandly
grandmother
grandness
grandparent
grandsire
grandson
grange
granite
graniverous
grant
granted
granular
granulate
granulated
granulation
granule
grape
grapeshot
graph
graphic
graphical
graphics
graphite
grapnel
grapple

grasp
graspingly
grass
grasshopper
grassplot
grate
grated
grateful
grater
gratification
gratify
gratingly
gratis
gratitude
gratuitous
gratuity
gravamen
grave
gravel
gravely
graven
graver
gravest
gravestone
gravitate
gravitated
gravitation
gravitational
gravity
gravy
gray

graybeard
grayish
grayness
graze
grazier
grease
greasewood
greasier
greasiest
greasily
greasiness
great
greatly
greatness
greed
greedier
greediest
greedily
greediness
greedy
Greek
green
greenback
greener
greenery
greenest
greenhorn
greenhouse
greenish
greenness
greenroom

greenwood
greet
greeted
greetings
gregarious
gregariously
Gregorian
grenade
grenadier
grenadine
grew
grid
griddle
gridiron
grief
grievance
grieve
grievous
grievously
grill
grilled
grim
grimace
grime
grimly
grimness
grimy
grin
grind
grinder
grindingly

grindstone
grinned
grip
gripe
gripper
grisly
grist
gristle
grit
grittiness
gritty
grizzle
grizzled
grizzly
groan
groaned
groaningly
grocer
grocery
grog
groin
grommet
groom
groomed
groove
grope
gropingly
grosgrain
gross
grosser
grossest

grossly
grossness
grotesque
grotesquely
grotto
grouch
grouchily
grouchy
ground
grounded
groundless
groundling
groundwork
group
groupings
grouse
grout
grove
grovel
groveled
grow
grower
growl
growled
grown
growth
grub
grubbiness
grubby
grudge
grudgingly

gruel
gruesome
gruff
gruffer
gruffest
gruffly
grumble
grumpiness
grumpy
grunt
grunted
guarantee
guaranteed
guarantor
guaranty
guard
guarded
guardian
guardianship
guardroom
guardsman
guava
gubernatorial
gudgeon
guerdon
guerrilla
guess
guesswork
guest
guidance
guide
guidebook
guided
guidepost
guidon
guild
guile
guileful
guileless
guillotine
guilt
guiltily
guiltless
guilty
guinea
guise
guises
guitar
gulch
gulden
gulf
gull
gullet
gullets
gullibility
gullible
gulp
gum
gumbo
gumboil
gummosis
gummy
gumption
gumshoe
gumwood
gun
gunboat
guncotton
gunfire
gunlock
gunman
gunner
gunnery
gunny
gunpaper
gunpowder
gunrunning
gunshop
gunshot
gunsmith
gunstock
gunwale
gurgle
gush
gusher
gushingly
gushy
gusset
gust
gustatory
gustily
gusto
gusty

gutter
gutteral
gutteralize
gutterally
gutteralness
guttersnipe
guy
guzzle
guzzled
guzzler
gymkhana
gymnasium
gymnast
gymnastic
gynecologist
gynecology
gypsum
gypsy
gyrate
gyration
gyratory
gyrfalcon
gyro
gyrocompass
gyroscope
gyrostat
gyves

H

haberdasher
haberdashery
habiliment
habit
habitable
habitant
habitat
habitation
habitual
habitually
habituate
habituated
habitude
hackle
hackman
hackneyed
hacksaw
had
haddock
hafnium
haft
hag
haggard
haggle
haggled
hail
hailed

hailstone
hailstorm
hair
hairbreadth
hairbrush
haircut
hairpin
hairsplitter
hairspring
hairy
halberd
halcyon
hale
half
halfway
halfwitted
halibut
halitosis
hall
hallow
Halloween
hallucination
hallucinatory
hallucinosis
halo
halogen
halt

halter
haltingly
halyard
ham
hamlet
hamlets
hammer
hammered
hammerless
hammock
hamper
hampered
hamster
hamstring
hand
handball
handbook
handcuff
handed
handful
handicap
handicraft
handier
handiest
handily
handiness
handiwork

handkerchief
handle
handled
handmade
handrail
handsome
handsomely
handspring
handwriting
handy
hang
hangar
hanged
hanger
hangman
hanker
hankered
hansom
haphazard
hapless
happen
happened
happenings
happier
happiest
happily
happiness
happy
harangue
harangued
harass

harassment
harbinger
harbor
harbored
hard
harden
hardened
hardener
harder
hardest
hardier
hardiest
hardihood
hardiness
hardly
hardness
hardship
hardware
hardy
hare
harebrained
harelip
harem
hark
Harlequin
harm
harmed
harmful
harmless
harmlessly
harmonic

harmonica
harmonious
harmoniously
harmonization
harmonize
harmonized
harmony
harness
harp
harpist
harpoon
harpooned
harpsichord
harrier
harrow
harsh
harsher
harshest
harshly
harshness
harvest
harvester
has
hash
hashish
hasp
hassock
haste
hasten
hastened
hastily

hastiness
hasty
hat
hatband
hatch
hatchery
hatchet
hatchment
hatchway
hate
hated
hateful
hatefully
hatefulness
hatred
hatter
haughtily
haughty
haul
haulage
hauled
haunch
haunt
haunted
hauntingly
have
haven
haversack
havoc
Hawaiian
hawk

hawker
hawkweed
hawse
hawser
hawthorn
hay
haycock
hayfork
hayloft
haymow
hayrack
hayseed
haystack
hazard
hazardous
hazardously
haze
hazel
hazily
haziness
hazy
he
head
headache
headband
headboard
headcheese
headdress
header
headfirst
headforemost

headgear
headily
headings
headland
headless
headlight
headline
headlock
headlong
headmaster
headpiece
headquarters
headsman
headspring
headstone
headstrong
headwater
headway
headwork
heady
heal
healed
healer
health
healthful
healthfulness
healthier
healthiest
healthily
healthy
heap

hear
heard
hearer
hearings
hearken
hearsay
hearse
heart
heartache
heartbeat
heartbreak
heartbroken
heartburn
hearten
heartfelt
hearth
hearthstone
heartier
heartiest
heartily
heartless
hearty
heat
heater
heath
heathen
heathenish
heathenism
heather
heave
heaven

heavenly
heavenward
heavier
heaviest
heavily
heaviness
heavy
Hebraic
Hebrew
hecatomb
heckle
heckled
hectic
hectograph
hedge
hedgehog
hedgerow
hedonism
heed
heeded
heedfully
heedfulness
heedless
heedlessness
heel
heft
hegemony
hegira
heifer
height
heighten

heinous
heir
heiress
heirloom
helical
helicoid
helicopter
heliotrope
helium
helix
helm
helmet
helmeted
helmsman
help
helper
helpful
helpfully
helpfulness
helpings
helpless
helplessly
helplessness
helpmate
hem
hematite
hemicycle
hemisphere
hemlock
hemorrhage
hemp

hemstitch
hence
henceforth
henceforward
henchman
henequen
henhouse
hepatalgia
hepatic
hepatica
hepatitis
hepatotomy
heptagon
heptameter
heptangular
herald
heraldic
heraldry
herb
herbaceous
herbage
herbal
herbarium
herbivorous
Herculean
herd
here
hereabouts
hereafter
hereby
hereditability
hereditable
hereditament
hereditary
heredity
hereinafter
hereinbefore
hereon
heresy
heretic
heretical
hereto
heretofore
hereunto
hereupon
herewith
heritability
heritable
heritably
heritage
hermetic
hermetically
hermit
hermitage
hernia
herniotomy
hero
heroic
heroical
heroine
heroism
heron
herpes
herpetology
herring
hers
herself
hesitance
hesitancy
hesitant
hesitate
hesitated
hesitatingly
hesitation
heterodox
heterogeneity
heterogeneous
hew
hewed
hexagon
hexagonal
hexameter
hexangular
hexapod
hiatus
hibernate
hibernation
hibiscus
hickory
hid
hidden
hide
hideous

hideously
hierarchy
hieratic
high
highborn
highboy
higher
highest
highland
highlander
highly
highness
highroad
highway
hike
hiker
hilarious
hilarity
hill
hillier
hilliest
hilliness
hillock
hillside
hilt
him
himself
hinder
hindered
hindrance
hinge

hint
hinted
hinterland
hintingly
hippodrome
hippopotamus
hippopotamuses
hire
hired
hireling
hirsute
his
hiss
histology
historian
historic
historical
history
histrionic
hit
hitch
hither
hitherto
hive
hoar
hoard
hoarded
hoarder
hoardings
hoarfrost
hoarse

hoarser
hoarsest
hoax
hobble
hobby
hobnail
hobnob
hobo
hock
hockey
hod
hoe
hog
hogback
hogfish
hoggish
hogshead
hoist
hokum
hold
holder
holdings
hole
holiday
holily
holiness
holland
hollow
hollowed
hollowness
holly

hollyhock
holocaust
holograph
holographic
holster
holy
holystone
homage
home
homeless
homelike
homeliness
homely
homeopathic
homeopathy
homesickness
homespun
homestead
homeward
homework
homicidal
homicide
homiletics
homilies
homily
hominy
homogeneity
homogeneous
homogenize
homologous
homonym
homunculus
hone
honest
honestly
honesty
honey
honeybee
honeycomb
honeydew
honeyed
honeymoon
honeysuckle
honk
honor
honorable
honorably
honorarium
honorary
honored
hood
hooded
hoodlum
hoodoo
hoodwink
hoof
hook
hooker
hookup
hookworm
hoop
Hoosier
hope
hopeful
hopefully
hopefulness
hopeless
hopelessly
hopelessness
hoplite
hopper
hopscotch
horde
horizon
horizontal
horizontally
hormone
horn
hornbook
horned
hornet
hornpipe
horology
horoscope
horrible
horrid
horrification
horrify
horror
horse
horseback
horsehair
horseman

horseshoe
horseweed
horsewhip
horsewoman
hortatory
horticulture
hose
hosier
hosiery
hospice
hospitable
hospital
hospitality
hospitalization
hospitalize
host
hostage
hostel
hostess
hostile
hostilely
hostility
hot
hotbed
hotel
hotheaded
hothouse
hotly
hotness
hotter
hottest

hound
hounded
hour
hourly
house
housed
housefly
household
householder
housekeeper
housemaid
houseroom
housetop
housewarming
housewife
housework
hovel
hover
how
however
howitzer
howl
howsoever
hub
hubbub
huckleberry
huckster
huddle
huddled
hue
huff

hug
huge
Huguenot
hulk
hull
hulled
hum
human
humane
humaneness
humanism
humanitarian
humanity
humanization
humanize
humanized
humankind
humanly
humble
humbled
humbleness
humbly
humbug
humdrum
humerus
humid
humidifier
humidify
humidity
humidor
humiliate

humiliated
humiliation
humility
hummed
hummock
humor
humored
humorist
humorous
humorousness
hump
humus
hunch
hundred
hundredth
hunger
hungered
hungrily
hungry
hunk
hunt
hunted
hunter
huntsman
hurdle
hurdled
hurl
hurled
hurricane
hurry
hurt

hurtful
hurtfully
hurtfulness
hurtle
hurtled
husband
husbandry
hush
hushed
husk
huskily
huskiness
husky
hussy
hustings
hustle
hustled
hustler
hutch
hyacinth
hyaloid
hybrid
hydrangea
hydrant
hydrate
hydraulic
hydrocarbon
hydrochloric
hydrocyanic
hydroelectric
hydrogen

hydrometer
hydrophobia
hydroplane
hydroponics
hydrostatics
hydroxide
hyena
hygiene
hygienic
hygienically
hymn
hymnal
hyperactive
hyperalgia
hyperbola
hyperbole
hypercritical
hyperemia
hyperopia
hypertension
hyperthyroid
hypertrophy
hyphen
hyphenate
hyphenated
hypnosis
hypnotism
hypnotist
hypnotize
hypochlorite
hypochondria

hypochondriac	hypotenuse	hypothetical
hypocrisy	hypothecate	hypothetically
hypocrite	hypotheses	hysteria
hypocritical	hypothesis	hysterical
hypodermic	hypothesize	hysterics
hypoglottis	hypothetic	hysteroid

I

iambic
Iberian
ibex
ibis
ice
iceberg
icebound
icehouse
iceman
ichneumon
ichor
ichthyology
icicle
icily
iciness
icy
icon
idea
ideal
idealism
idealist
idealistic
idealization
idealize
ideally
identical
identification

identify
identity
idiocy
idiom
idiomatic
idiosyncrasy
idiot
idiotic
idle
idled
idleness
idler
idly
idol
idolater
idolatrous
idolatry
idolize
idyl
idyllic
if
igloo
igneous
ignite
ignition
ignoble
ignominious

ignominy
ignoramus
ignorance
ignorant
ignorantly
ignore
iguana
ilex
Iliad
ilk
ill
illegal
illegality
illegibility
illegible
illegitimacy
illegitimate
illiberal
illicit
illimitable
illinium
illiteracy
illiterate
illness
illogical
illuminant
illuminate

illumination
illuminator
illumine
illusion
illusive
illusory
illustrate
illustrated
illustration
illustrative
illustrator
illustrious
image
imagery
imaginable
imaginary
imagination
imaginative
imagine
imaginings
imbecile
imbecility
imbibe
imbroglio
imbue
imitable
imitate
imitation
imitative
imitator
immaculate
immaculately
immanent
immaterial
immature
immaturely
immaturity
immeasurable
immediacy
immediate
immediately
immediateness
immemorial
immense
immensely
immensity
immerse
immersion
immigrant
immigration
imminence
imminent
immobile
immobility
immobilization
immobilize
immoderate
immodest
immolate
immolation
immoral
immorality
immorally
immortal
immortality
immortalize
immortally
immovability
immovable
immovableness
immovably
immune
immunity
immunization
immunize
immunology
immure
immutability
immutable
imp
impact
impaction
impair
impaired
impairment
impale
impaled
impalement
impalpability
impalpable
impalpably
impanel
impaneled

impart
imparted
impartial
impartiality
impartially
impassability
impasse
impassible
impassion
impassioned
impassive
impassively
impassivity
impatience
impatient
impeach
impeachable
impeachment
impeccability
impeccable
impeccant
impeccancy
impecuniosity
impecunious
impedance
impede
impediment
impedimenta
impel
impelled
impend

impenetrability
impenetrable
imperative
imperceptible
imperfect
imperfection
imperial
imperious
imperishable
impersonal
impersonate
impertinence
impertinent
imperturbable
impervious
impetigo
impetuosity
impetuous
impetuously
impetuousness
impetus
impiety
impinge
impingement
impious
impiously
impish
implacability
implacable
implant
implausible

implement
implicate
implication
implicit
implicitly
imploration
implore
imploringly
implied
imply
impolite
impolitely
impoliteness
impolitic
imponderable
import
importance
important
importation
importer
importunity
impose
imposingly
imposition
impossibility
impossible
impost
impostor
imposture
impotence
impotent

impound
impoverish
impoverishment
impower
impracticability
impracticable
imprecate
imprecation
imprecatory
impregnability
impregnable
impregnate
impregnation
impresario
imprescriptible
impress
impression
impressionable
impressionism
impressionistic
impressive
imprimatur
imprint
imprison
imprisoned
imprisonment
improbability
improbably
impromptu
improper
impropriety

improvable
improve
improvement
improvidence
improvident
improvisation
improvise
imprudence
imprudently
impudence
impudent
impudently
impugn
impugnable
impugned
impugnment
impulse
impulsion
impulsive
impunity
impure
impurely
impurity
imputable
imputation
imputative
impute
inability
inaccessibility
inaccessible
inaccuracy

inaccurate
inaction
inactive
inactivity
inadequacy
inadequate
inadmissibility
inadmissible
inadvertence
inadvertent
inadvisability
inadvisable
inalienable
inane
inanimate
inanition
inanity
inapplicable
inapposite
inappreciable
inappreciative
inappropriate
inapt
inaptitude
inarticulate
inartistic
inasmuch
inattention
inattentive
inaudibility
inaudible

inaudibly
inaugural
inaugurate
inauguration
inauspicious
inborn
inbred
incalculable
incandesce
incandescence
incandescent
incantation
incapable
incapacitate
incapacitation
incarcerate
incarceration
incarnate
incarnation
incendiarism
incendiary
incense
incentive
inception
incertitude
incessant
incessantly
incest
incestuous
inch
inchoate

inchworm
incidence
incident
incidental
incidentally
incinerate
incinerated
incineration
incinerator
incipient
incise
incised
incision
incisive
incisively
incisiveness
incisor
incitation
incite
incitement
incivility
inclemency
inclement
inclination
incline
inclined
inclose
inclosure
include
included
inclusive

inclusively
incognito
incoherence
incoherent
incombustibility
incombustible
income
incommensurable
incommensurate
incomparable
incompatibility
incompatible
incompetence
incompetent
incomplete
incomprehensibility
incomprehensible
incompressibility
incompressible
inconceivability
inconceivable
inconclusive
inconclusiveness
incongruity
incongruous
inconsequential
inconsiderable
inconsiderate
inconsiderately
inconsistency
inconsistent

inconsolable
inconspicuous
inconstancy
inconstant
incontestable
incontinence
incontinent
incontrovertible
inconvenience
inconvenient
inconveniently
inconvertibility
inconvertible
incorporate
incorporation
incorporator
incorrect
incorrigibility
incorrigible
incorruptibility
incorruptible
increase
increasingly
incredibility
incredible
incredulity
incredulous
increment
incriminate
incrimination
incriminatory

incrustation
incubate
incubation
incubator
incubus
inculcate
inculcation
inculpate
inculpation
inculpatory
incumbency
incumbent
incunabula
incur
incurable
incurably
incurred
incursion
indebtedness
indecency
indecent
indecently
indecision
indecisive
indecorous
indecorum
indeed
indefatigable
indefensible
indefinable
indefinite

indefiniteness
indelibility
indelible
indelicacy
indelicate
indelicately
indemnification
indemnify
indemnity
indent
indentation
indented
indention
indenture
independence
independent
indescribable
indestructible
indeterminable
indeterminate
index
indexed
indexer
indexes
Indian
indicate
indication
indicative
indicator
indicatory
indices

indicia
indict
indictable
indictment
indifference
indifferent
indifferently
indigence
indigenous
indigent
indigestibility
indigestible
indignant
indignantly
indignation
indignity
indigo
indirect
indirection
indirectly
indirectness
indiscreet
indiscretion
indiscriminate
indispensability
indispensable
indispose
indisposed
indisposition
indisputable
indissoluble

indistinct
indistinctly
indistinguishable
indite
indium
individual
individualism
individualist
individualistic
individuality
individualize
individually
indivisibility
indivisible
indoctrinate
indoctrination
indolence
indolent
indomitable
indoors
indorse
indorsee
indorsement
indorser
indubitable
induce
inducement
induct
inductance
inducted
induction

inductive
inductor
indulge
indulgence
indulgent
indurate
industrial
industrialism
industrialist
industrialization
industrialize
industrially
industrious
industriousness
industry
inebriate
inebriation
inebriety
inedible
ineffable
ineffably
ineffective
ineffectual
ineffectually
inefficacious
inefficiency
inefficient
inefficiently
inelastic
inelasticity
inelegance

inelegant
ineligibility
ineligible
ineluctable
inept
ineptitude
inequality
inequitable
inequity
ineradicable
ineradicably
inerrancy
inerrant
inert
inertia
inertly
inertness
inessential
inestimable
inestimably
inevitability
inevitable
inevitably
inexact
inexactitude
inexcusable
inexhaustible
inexhaustibly
inexorable
inexpedience
inexpediency

inexpedient
inexpensive
inexperience
inexperienced
inexpert
inexplicable
inexplicably
inextricable
infallibility
infallible
infamous
infamy
infancy
infant
infanticide
infantile
infantilism
infantry
infarct
infarction
infatuate
infatuated
infatuation
infeasible
infect
infected
infection
infectious
infectiously
infectiousness
infelicitous

infelicity
infer
inference
inferential
inferior
inferiority
infernal
infernally
inferno
inferred
infertile
infertility
infest
infestation
infidel
infidelity
infield
infielder
infiltrate
infiltration
infinite
infinitesimal
infinitesimally
infinitive
infinitude
infinity
infirm
infirmary
infirmity
inflame
inflamed

inflammability	infrequent	inhabitance
inflammable	infrequently	inhabitancy
inflammably	infringe	inhabitation
inflammation	infringed	inhabited
inflammatory	infringement	inhalation
inflate	infuriate	inhale
inflated	infuriated	inhaled
inflation	infuse	inhaler
inflationary	infused	inharmonious
inflect	infuses	inhere
inflection	infusion	inhered
inflexibility	ingenious	inherence
inflexible	ingeniously	inherent
inflict	ingenuity	inherently
infliction	ingenuous	inherit
influence	ingest	inheritable
influential	ingestion	inheritance
influenza	inglorious	inherited
influx	ingot	inheritor
inform	ingrain	inhibit
informal	ingrained	inhibited
informality	ingratiate	inhibition
informant	ingratiated	inhibitory
information	ingratiation	inhospitable
informative	ingratiatory	inhospitably
informed	ingratitude	inhuman
informer	ingredient	inhumane
informingly	ingress	inhumanity
infraction	ingrown	inimical
infrangible	inhabit	inimitable
infrared	inhabitable	inimitably

iniquitous
iniquitously
iniquity
initial
initialed
initially
initiate
initiated
initiation
initiative
initiator
initiatory
inject
injected
injection
injector
injudicious
injudiciously
injunction
injure
injured
injurious
injury
injustice
injustices
ink
inked
inkhorn
inkling
inklings
inkstand
inkwell
inky
inlaid
inland
inlay
inlet
inlets
inmate
inmost
inn
innate
innately
inner
innermost
inning
innings
innkeeper
innocence
innocent
innocently
innocuous
innocuously
innovate
innovation
innovative
innovator
innuendo
innumerable
inobservant
inoculate
inoculated
inoculation
inoffensive
inoperable
inoperative
inopportune
inordinate
inorganic
inpatient
inquest
inquietude
inquire
inquired
inquirer
inquires
inquiries
inquiringly
inquiry
inquisition
inquisitive
inquisitor
inquisitorial
inroad
insane
insanely
insanitary
insanitation
insanity
insatiability
insatiable
inscribe
inscriber

inscription
inscrutability
inscrutable
insect
insecticide
insectivorous
insecure
insecurity
insensate
insensibility
insensible
insensitive
insensitiveness
insentience
insentient
inseparable
inseparably
insert
inserted
insertion
inset
inshore
inside
insider
insides
insidious
insidiously
insight
insigne
insignia
insignificance
insignificant
insincere
insincerely
insincerity
insinuate
insinuated
insinuatingly
insinuation
insipid
insipidity
insipidly
insist
insisted
insistence
insistent
insobriety
insole
insolence
insolent
insolently
insolubility
insoluble
insolvable
insolvency
insolvent
insomnia
insomuch
insouciance
inspect
inspection
inspector
inspiration
inspirational
inspiratory
inspire
inspired
inspirer
inspiringly
inspiritingly
instability
install
installation
installed
installment
instance
instant
instantaneous
instanter
instantly
instate
instead
instep
instigate
instigated
instigation
instigator
instill
instilled
instinct
instinctive
instinctively
institute

instituted
institution
institutional
instruct
instruction
instructional
instructive
instructor
instrument
instrumental
instrumentalist
instrumentality
instrumentally
instrumentation
insubordinate
insubordination
insufferable
insufficiency
insufficient
insular
insularity
insulate
insulated
insulation
insulator
insulin
insult
insulted
insultingly
insuperable
insupportable

insuppressible
insurability
insurable
insurance
insure
insured
insurer
insurgency
insurgent
insurmountable
insurrection
insurrectionary
insurrectionist
intact
intaglio
intake
intangibility
intangible
integer
integral
integrally
integrate
integrated
integration
integrity
integument
intellect
intellectual
intellectualize
intellectually
intelligence

intelligent
intelligibility
intelligible
intemperance
intemperate
intemperately
intend
intendant
intended
intense
intensification
intensifier
intensify
intensity
intensive
intent
intention
intentional
intentionally
intently
intentness
interact
interaction
interborough
interbreed
intercede
interceded
intercept
intercepted
interception
interceptor

intercession
intercessory
interchange
interchangeability
interchangeable
intercollegiate
intercommunicate
interconnect
intercostal
intercourse
interdenominational
interdependent
interdependence
interdict
interdiction
interest
interested
interestedly
interestingly
interfere
interfered
interference
interferingly
interim
interior
interject
interjection
interlace
interlaced
interlard
interleaf

interleave
interline
interlineal
interlinear
interlineation
interlined
interlobar
interlock
interlocked
interlocutor
interlocutory
interloper
interlude
intermarriage
intermarry
intermediary
intermediate
interment
intermezzo
interminable
interminably
intermingle
intermingled
intermission
intermit
intermittence
intermittent
intermittently
intermixture
intern
internal

internally
international
internationalize
internationally
interne
internecine
internment
interpellate
interpellation
interplanetary
interpolate
interpolated
interpolation
interpose
interposition
interpret
interpretation
interpretative
interpreted
interpreter
interregnum
interrelation
interrogate
interrogation
interrogative
interrogatory
interrupt
interruptedly
interruption
interscapular
interscholastic

intersect
intersperse
interstate
interstellar
interstice
interstices
interstitial
interstitially
intertwine
interval
intervene
intervened
intervention
interview
interviewed
interviewer
interweave
interwoven
intestacy
intestate
intestinal
intestine
intimacy
intimate
intimated
intimately
intimation
intimidate
intimidated
intimidation
into

intolerable
intolerance
intolerant
intonation
intone
intoned
intoxicant
intoxicate
intoxicated
intoxication
intractability
intractable
intramural
intransigence
intransigent
intransitive
intrastate
intrenchment
intrepid
intrepidity
intrepidly
intricacies
intricacy
intricate
intricately
intrigue
intrigued
intrinsic
introduce
introduced
introduction

introductory
introit
introspect
introspection
introspective
introversion
introvert
intrude
intruded
intruder
intrusion
intrusive
intrusively
intuition
intuitive
intuitively
inunction
inundate
inundated
inundation
inure
invade
invaded
invalid
invalidate
invalidated
invalidation
invalidity
invaluable
invar
invariability

invariable
invariableness
invasion
invective
inveigh
inveigle
inveigled
invent
invention
inventive
inventively
inventiveness
inventor
inventory
inverse
inversion
invert
inverted
invertible
invest
invested
investigate
investigated
investigation
investigative
investigator
investiture
investment
investor
invests
inveterate

invidious
invidiously
invigorate
invigorated
invigoration
invincibility
invincible
inviolability
inviolable
inviolate
invisibility
invisible
invitation
invite
invited
invitingly
invocation
invoice
invoices
invoke
invoked
involuntarily
involuntary
involute
involution
involve
involved
invulnerability
invulnerable
inward
inwardly

inwardness
iodate
iodic
iodide
iodine
iodize
ion
Ionic
ionization
ionize
iota
ipecac
Iranian
irascibility
irascible
irate
irately
iridectomy
iridescence
iridescent
iridium
iris
Irish
Irishman
iritis
irk
irksome
iron
ironclad
ironed
ironical

ironside
ironware
ironwood
ironwork
irony
Iroquois
irradiate
irradiated
irradiation
irrational
irrationally
irreconcilability
irreconcilable
irrecoverable
irredeemable
irreducible
irrefragable
irrefrangible
irrefutable
irregular
irregularity
irrelevance
irrelevant
irreligious
irremediable
irremovable
irreparable
irreplaceable
irrepressible
irreproachable
irresistible

irresolute
irresolution
irrespective
irresponsibility
irresponsible
irretraceable
irretrievable
irreverence
irreverent
irreversible
irrevocable
irrigable
irrigate
irrigated
irrigation
irritability
irritable
irritant
irritate
irritated
irritation
irritative
irruption
ischium
isinglass
Islam
island
islander
isle
isobar
isolate

isolation
isolationist
isomer
isomeric
isotherm
issuance
issue
issued
issues
isthmus
it
Italian
Italianate
italic
italicize
itch
itchier
itchiest
itchy
item
itemize
itemized
iterate
itineracy
itinerancy
itinerant
itinerary
itinerate
its
itself
ivory

J

jabber
jabot
jack
jackal
jackanapes
jackdaw
jacket
jackknife
jackstraw
Jacobean
jade
jadeite
jaguar
jail
jailed
jailer
jam
jamboree
jammed
jangle
janitor
janitress
January
japan
Japanese
jar
jargon
jarred
jasmine
jasper
jaundice
jaunt
jauntier
jauntiest
jauntily
jauntiness
jaunty
javelin
jawbone
jealous
jealousy
jeer
jeeringly
Jehovah
jejune
jellied
jelly
jellyfish
jeopardize
jeopardy
jeremiad
jerk
jerkily
jerky
jersey
jest
jester
jestingly
Jesuit
Jesus
jet
jetsam
jettison
jetty
jewel
jeweled
jeweler
jewelry
Jewish
Jewry
jibe
jig
jigger
jiggle
jiggled
jigsaw
jingle
jingled
jingo
jingoism
jinrikisha

jinx
jitney
job
jobber
jockey
jocose
jocosely
jocosity
jocular
jocularity
jocularly
jocund
jocundity
jog
jogged
joggle
join
joinder
joined
joiner
joinings
joint
jointed
jointly
jointure
joist
joke
joker
jokingly
jollification
jollity

jolly
jonquil
jostle
jostled
jot
jounce
journal
journalism
journalist
journalize
journey
journeyed
jovial
joviality
jovially
jowl
joy
joyful
joyfully
joyfulness
joyless
joyous
jubilance
jubilant
jubilate
jubilation
jubilee
judge
judged
judgeship
judgment

judicative
judicatory
judicature
judicial
judicially
judiciary
judicious
juggle
juggled
juggler
jugular
juice
juicy
julep
July
jumble
jumbo
jump
jumper
junction
juncture
June
jungle
junior
juniper
junk
junket
jurat
juridical
jurisconsult
jurisdiction

jurisprudence
jurist
juror
jury
juryman
just
justice
justifiable
justification
justificatory
justified
justify
justly
justness
jute
juvenile
juvenility
juxtaposition

K

kaiser
kale
kaleidoscope
kaleidoscopic
kangaroo
kaolin
kapok
karma
kava
kayak
keel
keen
keenly
keenness
keep
keeper
keg
kelp
kennel
kept
keratin
kerchief
kernel
kerosene
kersey
kestrel
ketch
ketosis
kettle
key
keyboard
keyed
khaki
khedive
kibitzer
kick
kicker
kid
kidnap
kidnaped
kidney
kilerg
kill
killed
killer
killings
kiln
kilocycle
kilogram
kilometer
kilt
kilted
kin
kind
kinder
kindest
kindle
kindled
kindliness
kindly
kindness
kindred
kine
kinesthetic
kinetic
king
kingbird
kingbolt
kingcraft
kingdom
kingfish
kingfisher
kinglet
kinglets
kingliness
kingly
kingpin
kingship
kink
kinship
kinsman

kiosk
kipper
kitchen
kitchenette
kite
kith
kitten
kleptomania
kleptomaniac
klieg
knapsack
knave
knavery
knavish
kneecap
kneel
kneeled
knelt
knew
knickers
knickknack
knife

knifed
knight
knighted
knighthood
knightliness
knightly
knights
knit
knitter
knives
knob
knock
knockdown
knocker
knockout
knoll
knot
knothole
knotted
knotty
knout
know

knowable
knowingly
knowingness
knowledge
known
knuckle
knuckled
knurl
knurled
knurly
kobold
kodak
kohlrabi
kopeck
Koran
kosher
kraft
kremlin
kulak
krypton
kymograph
kyphosis

L

label
labeled
labial
labor
laboratory
labored
laborer
laborious
laboriously
laburnum
labyrinth
lace
laced
lacerate
lacerated
laceration
laches
lachrymal
lachrymose
lacings
lack
lackey
laconic
lacquer
lacquered
lacrosse
lactate

lactation
lacteal
lactic
lactose
lacuna
lacunae
ladder
laden
ladle
ladled
lady
ladylike
ladyship
lag
laggard
lagged
lagoon
lair
laird
laity
lake
lambdoid
lambent
lambkin
lamblike
lambrequin
lame

lamed
lamely
lameness
lament
lamentable
lamentation
lamented
lamina
laminate
laminated
lamination
lampoon
lamprey
lance
lancer
lancet
lancinating
lancination
land
landau
landed
landfall
landholder
landlady
landlocked
landlord
landmark

landscape
landslip
landsman
landward
language
languid
languish
languishingly
languor
languorous
lanky
lanolin
lansdowne
lantern
lanthanum
lanyard
lap
lapel
lapful
lapidary
lapse
lapsed
lapwing
larboard
larcenous
larceny
larch
lard
large
largely
largeness
larger
largess
largest
lariat
lark
larkspur
larva
larvae
larval
laryngeal
laryngitis
larynx
lascar
lascivious
lash
lashed
lashings
lassitude
lasso
last
lasted
lastingly
lastly
lasts
Latakia
latch
latched
latchkey
latchstring
late
lateen
lately
latency
lateness
latent
later
lateral
laterally
latest
lath
lather
laths
Latin
Latinism
Latinity
latitude
latitudinal
latitudinarian
latter
lattermost
lattice
latticework
laud
laudability
laudable
laudanum
laudation
laudatory
laugh
laughable
laughingly
laughingstock

laughter
launch
launchings
launder
laundered
laundress
laundry
laundryman
laureate
laurel
lava
lavalliere
lavatory
lavender
lavish
law
lawbreaker
lawful
lawfully
lawgiver
lawless
lawlessness
lawmaker
lawn
lawsuit
lawyer
lax
laxative
laxity
laxly
laxness

layer
layman
lazaretto
lazier
laziest
lazily
laziness
lazy
leach
lead
leaden
leader
leadership
leadsman
leaf
leaflet
leaflets
league
leagued
leak
leakage
leakiness
leaky
lean
leaned
leanings
leap
learn
learned
learnt
lease

leased
leasehold
leaseholder
leash
least
leather
leatheret
leathern
leatheroid
leathery
leave
leaven
leavings
lecithin
lectern
lecture
lectured
lecturer
ledger
leech
leek
leer
leered
leeringly
leeward
leeway
left
left-handed
leg
legacy
legal

legalism
legalistic
legality
legalization
legalize
legally
legate
legatee
legation
legato
legend
legendary
legerdemain
leggings
legibility
legible
legion
legionary
legislate
legislation
legislative
legislator
legislature
legitimacy
legitimate
legitimately
legitimateness
legitimation
legitimatize
legitimist
legume

leguminous
leisure
leisureliness
leisurely
lemon
lemonade
lemur
lend
length
lengthen
lengthened
lengthily
lengthiness
lengthways
lengthwise
lengthy
lenience
leniency
lenient
leniently
lenitive
lenity
lens
Lent
Lenten
lenticular
lentigo
lentil
lentoid
leonine
leopard

leper
leprosy
leprous
lesion
less
lessee
lessen
lessened
lesser
lesson
lest
let
lethal
lethargic
lethargical
lethargy
lets
letter
lettered
letterhead
letterpress
letters
lettuce
leucocyte
leucocytosis
leucoderma
leukemia
levant
levee
level
leveled

leveler
lever
leverage
levitate
levitation
levity
levulose
levy
lexicography
lexicon
liability
liable
liana
liar
libation
libel
libeled
libelant
libelee
libeler
libelous
liberal
liberalism
liberality
liberalization
liberalize
liberally
liberate
liberation
liberator
liberty

librarian
library
libretto
lice
license
licensee
licentiate
licentious
licentiousness
lichen
licit
lick
licorice
lictor
lie
liege
lien
lieu
lieutenancy
lieutenant
life
lifeguard
lifeless
lifelike
lifelong
lifetime
lifework
lift
ligament
ligate
ligation

ligature
ligatured
light
lighted
lighten
lightened
lighter
lighterage
lightest
lightheaded
lighthouse
lightly
lightness
lightning
lightship
lightweight
ligneous
lignify
lignite
likable
like
liked
likelihood
likely
liken
likeness
likewise
likings
lilac
liliaceous
lilt

liltingly
lily
limb
limber
limbo
lime
limekiln
limelight
limen
Limerick
limestone
limewater
liminal
limit
limitable
limitation
limited
limitless
limnology
limousine
limp
limpet
limpid
limpidity
limpidly
limply
limpness
linden
line
lineage
lineal
lineament
linear
lineman
linen
liner
linger
lingered
lingerie
lingo
lingual
linguist
linguistic
linguistically
linguistics
liniment
linings
link
linkage
linnet
linoleum
linotype
linseed
lint
lintel
lion
lioness
lionize
lipoid
lipoma
liquefaction
liquefiable
liquefy
liquescence
liquescent
liquid
liquidate
liquidated
liquidation
liquidator
liquor
lira
lisp
lispingly
lissome
list
listed
listen
listened
listener
listings
listless
litany
liter
literacy
literal
literalism
literality
literalize
literally
literary
literate
literature

litharge
lithe
lithesome
lithia
lithium
lithographer
lithographic
lithography
lithosis
lithotomy
Lithuania
litigable
litigant
litigate
litigation
litigious
litmus
litter
littered
little
littlest
littoral
liturgical
liturgy
livable
live
live
lived
liveliest
livelihood
liveliness
livelong
lively
liver
livery
livid
livings
lizard
llama
llano
load
loaded
loadings
loaf
loafer
loam
loan
loaned
loathe
loathed
loathful
loathly
loathsome
loaves
lobar
lobby
lobbyist
lobster
local
localism
locality
localization
localize
locally
locate
location
loci
lock
lockage
locker
locket
lockjaw
lockout
locksmith
lockup
locomotion
locomotive
locus
locust
locution
lode
lodestar
lodge
lodger
lodgings
lodgment
loft
loftily
loftiness
lofty
log
loganberry
logarithm

loggia
logic
logical
logician
logistics
logotype
logwood
loin
loiter
loitered
loiterer
loll
lolled
lollipop
lone
loneliness
lonely
lonesome
lonesomely
lonesomeness
long
longboat
longed
longer
longest
longevity
longhand
longhorn
longingly
longings
longitude
longitudinal
longshoreman
look
lookout
loom
loomed
loon
loony
loop
loophole
loose
loosely
loosen
loosened
looseness
looser
loosest
loot
lop
lopsided
loquacious
loquaciously
loquacity
lord
lordliness
lordly
lordosis
lordship
lore
lorgnette
losable
lose
loses
losings
loss
lost
lotion
lottery
lotus
loud
louder
loudest
loudly
loudness
lounge
louse
lout
loutish
louver
lovable
love
loveless
loveliness
lovelorn
lovely
lover
lovesick
lovingly
low
lowborn
lowboy
lowbred

lower
lowermost
lowest
lowland
lowliness
lowly
lowness
loyal
loyalist
loyally
loyalty
lozenge
lubricant
lubricate
lubrication
lubricator
lucent
lucid
lucidity
lucidly
luck
luckily
luckiness
luckless
lucky
lucrative
lucre
lucubration
ludicrous

lug
luggage
lugger
lugubrious
lukewarm
lull
lullaby
lulled
lumbago
lumber
luminary
luminescent
luminiferous
luminosity
luminous
lump
lumpy
lunacy
lunar
lunatic
lunch
luncheon
lunette
lung
lunge
lurch
lurched
lure
lurid

lurk
luscious
lush
lust
luster
lustful
lustily
lustiness
lustrous
lustrously
lustrum
lusty
lute
luxuriance
luxuriant
luxuriate
luxurious
luxury
lyceum
lyddite
lymph
lymphatic
lymphoid
lynx
lyonnaise
lyre
lyric
lyrical
lyricism

M

macabre
macadam
macadamize
macaroni
macaroon
macaw
macerate
maceration
Mach
machete
machicolation
machinate
machination
machine
machined
machinery
machinist
mackerel
macrocosm
macron
maculate
madam
madder
maddest
madhouse
madly
madman
madness
madrigal
maffia
magazine
magenta
maggot
Magi
magic
magical
magician
magisterial
magistracy
magistral
magistrate
magistrature
magnanimous
magnate
magnesia
magnesium
magnet
magnetic
magnetically
magnetism
magnetization
magnetize
magneto
magnification
magnificence
magnificent
magnifico
magnifier
magnify
magniloquent
magnitude
magnolia
magnum
magpie
maguey
maharajah
mahatma
mahogany
maid
maiden
maidenhair
maidenhood
maidenly
maidservant
mail
mailability
mailable
mailed
mailer
mailings
maim

maimed
main
mainland
mainly
mainmast
mainsail
mainsheet
mainspring
mainstay
maintain
maintainable
maintenance
majestic
majesty
majolica
major
majored
majority
majuscule
make
make-believe
maker
makeshift
makings
malachite
maladjustment
maladminister
maladroit
malady
malapert
malapropos

malaria
malarial
malassimilation
Malay
malcontent
male
malediction
maledictory
malefactor
maleficence
maleficent
malevolence
malevolent
malfeasance
malformed
malice
malicious
maliciously
maliciousness
malign
malignancy
malignant
malignantly
maligned
malignity
malignly
malinger
malingerer
mallard
malleability
malleable

malleolar
malleolus
mallet
malmsey
malnutrition
malodorous
malposition
malpractice
malt
Maltese
maltose
maltreat
malversation
mammal
mammon
mammoth
man
manacle
manage
manageability
manageable
manageably
management
manager
managerial
managerially
managership
manatee
mandamus
mandarin
mandate

mandated
mandatory
mandible
mandibular
mandolin
mandrake
mandrel
maneuver
maneuvered
manganate
manganese
manger
mangily
manginess
mangle
mangled
mango
mangrove
mangy
manhole
manhood
mania
maniac
maniacal
manicure
manicurist
manifest
manifestation
manifestly
manifesto
manifests

manifold
manifolder
manikin
manipulate
manipulated
manipulates
manipulation
manipulative
manipulator
manipulatory
mankind
manlike
manliness
manly
manna
manner
mannered
mannerism
mannerly
mannish
manometer
manometric
manor
manorial
mansard
manservant
mansion
manslaughter
manteau
mantel
mantilla

mantis
mantle
manual
manually
manufactory
manufacture
manufactured
manufacturer
manumission
manure
manuscript
Manx
many
map
maple
mapped
mar
marabou
maraschino
maraud
marauder
marble
March
marcher
marchioness
marconigram
mare
margarine
margin
marginal
marginalia

marginally
margrave
marigold
marinate
marinated
marination
marine
mariner
marionette
Marist
marital
maritime
marjoram
mark
marked
markedly
marker
market
marketability
marketable
markings
marksman
marl
marlin
marmalade
marmoset
marmot
maroon
marooned
marplot
marquisette

marred
marriage
marriageable
married
marrow
marrowbone
marrowfat
marrowy
marry
Mars
marshal
marshaled
marshiness
marshmallow
marshy
marsupial
mart
marten
martial
martially
martinet
martyr
martyrdom
marvel
marveled
marvelous
mascara
mascot
masculine
masculinity
mash

mashed
masher
mashie
mask
masked
masker
mason
masonic
masonry
masquerade
mass
massacre
massage
massive
mast
master
mastered
masterful
masterfully
masterfulness
masterly
masterpiece
mastership
masterwork
mastery
masthead
mastic
masticate
mastication
masticatory
mastiff

mastodon
mastoid
mastoiditis
mat
matador
match
matchless
matchlessly
matchmaker
matchwood
material
materialism
materialist
materialistic
materiality
materialization
materialize
materialized
materially
maternal
maternally
maternity
mathematician
mathematics
matinee
matriarch
matriarchy
matrices
matricide
matriculate
matriculated
matriculates
matriculation
matrimonial
matrimonially
matrimony
matrix
matron
matronly
matter
mattock
mattress
maturation
mature
matured
maturely
matureness
maturity
matutinal
maudlin
maul
mauled
mausoleum
mauve
maverick
mavis
mawkish
maxillary
maxim
maximal
maximize
maximum
May
mayhem
mayonnaise
mayor
mayoralty
mazurka
meadow
meager
meal
mealtime
mean
meander
meaningless
meaningly
meanings
meanly
meanness
meantime
meanwhile
measles
measurable
measurably
measure
measured
measureless
measurement
measurer
meat
meatus
mechanic
mechanical

mechanically
mechanician
mechanics
mechanism
mechanization
mechanize
medal
medalist
medalists
medallion
meddle
meddled
meddler
meddlesome
media
medial
median
mediate
mediated
mediation
mediative
mediator
medical
medically
medicament
medicate
medication
medicative
medicinal
medicinally
medicine

medieval
medievally
mediocre
mediocrity
meditate
meditated
meditation
meditative
medium
mediums
medlar
meek
meekly
meekness
meerschaum
meet
meetings
megacycle
megaphone
meiosis
melancholia
melancholic
melancholy
melanosis
meliorate
melioration
mellifluous
mellow
melodeon
melodic
melodious

melodiously
melodrama
melodramatic
melody
melon
melt
meltable
melted
meltingly
member
membership
membrane
membranous
memento
memoir
memorabilia
memorable
memoranda
memorandum
memorandums
memorial
memorization
memorize
memory
menace
menage
menagerie
mend
mendacious
mendacity
mended

mendicancy
mendicant
menhaden
menial
menially
meningitis
mensuration
mensurative
mental
mentality
mentally
menthol
mention
mentioned
mentor
menu
mephitic
mercantile
mercenary
mercerize
merchandise
merchant
merchantman
merciful
merciless
mercilessly
mercurial
mercury
mercy
mere
merely

merest
meretricious
merge
merger
meridian
meringue
merino
merit
merited
meritorious
meritoriously
mermaid
merrily
merriment
merry
merrymaking
mesa
mescal
mesh
mesmerism
mesmerize
message
messenger
Messiah
messmate
metabolic
metabolism
metacarpal
metacarpus
metal
metallic

metalloid
metallurgic
metallurgical
metallurgy
metamorphose
metamorphosis
metaphor
metaphorical
metaphysical
metaphysician
metaphysics
metastasis
metatarsus
meteor
meteoric
meteorite
meteoroid
meteorology
meter
methane
method
methodical
methodist
methodize
methodology
methyl
meticulous
metonymy
metric
metrical
metrology

metronome
metropolis
metropolitan
mettle
mettlesome
mezzanine
miasma
miasmal
miasmatic
mica
micaceous
microbe
microbiology
microcephalus
microcosm
microfilm
micrometer
micron
microorganism
microphone
microscope
microscopic
microtome
Midas
middle
middleman
middleweight
midge
midget
midiron
midland

midmost
midnight
midriff
midshipman
midst
midstream
midsummer
midway
midweek
midwife
midwinter
midyear
might
mightily
mightiness
mighty
migraine
migrate
migration
migratory
mikado
milch
mild
milder
mildest
mildew
mildly
mildness
mile
mileage
milepost

miler
milestone
miliary
militancy
militant
militarism
militarist
militaristic
military
militate
militated
militia
milk
milkings
milkman
milkweed
milky
mill
milled
millenary
millennial
millennium
miller
milline
milliner
millinery
million
millionaire
millionth
millpond
millstone

millwright
Miltonic
mime
mimeograph
mimetic
mimic
mimicry
mimosa
minaret
minatory
mince
mincingly
mind
minded
mindful
mine
miner
mineral
mineralogy
mingle
mingled
miniature
minim
minimal
minimization
minimize
minimum
minion
minister
ministered
ministerial
ministerially
ministration
ministry
mink
minnow
minor
minority
minster
minstrel
minstrelsy
mint
minuend
minus
minuscule
minute
minute
minuteness
minutia
minutiae
minx
miracle
miraculous
mirage
mire
mired
mirror
mirth
mirthful
mirthfully
mirthless
misadventure
misalliance
misanthrope
misanthropic
misanthropical
misanthropist
misanthropy
misapplication
misapply
misapprehension
misappropriate
misappropriation
misarrange
misbegotten
misbehave
misbehavior
miscalculate
miscall
miscarriage
miscarry
miscegenation
miscellanea
miscellaneous
miscellanist
miscellany
mischance
mischief
mischievous
miscible
misconceive
misconception
misconduct

misconstruction
misconstrue
miscount
miscreant
misdate
misdeal
misdeed
misdemeanor
misdirect
misdirection
misdoubt
miser
miserable
miserliness
miserly
misery
misfeasance
misfire
misfit
misformed
misfortune
misgivings
misgovern
misguide
mishap
misinform
misinformed
misinterpret
misinterpretation
misinterpreted
misjudge

misjudged
mislay
mislead
misleadingly
mislike
mismade
mismanage
mismate
misname
misnamed
misnomer
misplace
misprint
misprision
mispronounce
mispronunciation
misquotation
misquote
misread
misreadings
misremember
misrepresent
misrepresentation
misrule
miss
missile
mission
missionary
missive
misspell
misspelled

misspellings
misspent
misstate
misstatement
mistake
mistaken
mistakenly
misteach
mistiness
mistletoe
mistook
mistranslate
mistranslation
mistreat
mistreatment
mistress
mistrial
mistrust
mistrustful
misty
misunderstand
misunderstood
misuse
mite
miter
mitered
mitigable
mitigate
mitigation
mitosis
mitral

mitten
mix
mixed
mixer
mixture
mnemonic
moan
moaned
moat
mob
mobile
mobility
mobilization
mobilize
mobilized
moccasin
Mocha
mock
mockery
mockingly
modal
modality
mode
model
modeled
moderate
moderated
moderately
moderateness
moderation
moderator

modern
modernism
modernist
modernity
modernize
modernized
modest
modestly
modesty
modicum
modification
modified
modifier
modify
modish
modishly
modishness
modulate
modulated
modulates
modulation
modulator
module
modulus
mohair
Mohammedan
moiety
moist
moisten
moistened
moistener

moisture
molar
molasses
mold
molded
moldy
mole
molecular
molecule
molehill
molest
molestation
molests
mollification
mollify
mollusk
molt
molten
molybdenum
moment
momentarily
momentary
momently
momentous
momentum
monarch
monarchial
monarchism
monarchist
monarchistic
monarchy

monastery
monastic
monasticism
Monday
monetary
monetization
monetize
money
moneyed
mongoose
mongrel
monitor
monitored
monk
monkey
monocle
monody
monogamous
monogamy
monogram
monograph
monolith
monologue
monomania
monoplane
monopolism
monopolist
monopolistic
monopolization
monopolize
monopoly

monosyllabic
monosyllable
monotone
monotonous
monotony
monotype
monoxide
monsoon
monster
monstrance
monstrosity
monstrous
month
monthly
monument
monumental
monumentally
mood
moodily
moodiness
moody
moon
moonbeam
moonfish
moonlight
moonshine
moonstone
moonstruck
moor
moored
moorings

moorish
moose
moot
mop
moraine
moral
morale
moralist
moralistic
moralists
morality
moralization
moralize
moralized
morally
morass
moratorium
moray
morbid
morbidity
morbidly
mordant
more
moreover
morgue
Mormon
morning
mornings
morocco
moron
morose

morosely
morphine
morphinism
morphology
morris
morsel
mortal
mortality
mortally
mortar
mortgage
mortgagee
mortgagor
mortification
mortify
mortise
mortmain
mortuary
Moslem
mosque
mosquito
moss
mossback
mossiness
mossy
most
mostly
motet
moth
mother
motherhood

mother-in-law
motherland
motherless
motherliness
motherly
mother-of-pearl
motif
motion
motioned
motionless
motivate
motivation
motive
motley
motor
motored
motorist
motorists
motorman
mottle
mottled
motto
mound
mount
mountain
mountaineer
mountainous
mountebank
mounted
mountings
mourn

mourned
mourner
mournful
mouse
mouser
mousse
mouth
mouthed
mouthful
mouthpiece
movability
movable
move
moved
movement
mover
movie
movingly
mow
mow
mower
much
mucilage
mucilaginous
muck
mucoid
mucosa
mucous
mucus
mud
muddier

muddiest
muddily
muddiness
muddle
muddled
muddy
mudfish
muff
muffin
muffle
muffled
muffler
mufti
mug
mugginess
muggy
mulatto
mulberry
mulch
mulct
mulcted
mule
muleteer
mullion
multifarious
multifold
multiform
multiformity
multigraph
multilith
multimillionaire
multiple
multiplex
multiplicand
multiplicate
multiplication
multiplicative
multiplicity
multiplier
multiply
multitude
multitudinous
multivalent
mumble
mumbled
mummer
mummery
mummification
mummify
mummy
mumps
munch
mundane
municipal
municipality
municipally
munificence
munificent
muniment
munition
mural
murder
murdered
murderer
murderous
muriatic
murk
murkily
murkiness
murky
murmur
murmured
murmurer
murmurous
muscadine
muscatel
muscle
muscular
muscularity
muscularly
musculature
muse
mused
museum
mush
mushroom
mushy
music
musical
musicale
musician
musicianly
musk

musket	muteness	myeloid
musketeer	mutilate	myoma
musketry	mutilated	myopia
muskmelon	mutilation	myopic
muskrat	mutilator	myosis
muslin	mutineer	myotic
muss	mutinous	myotomy
mussed	mutiny	myriad
mussel	mutter	myrrh
mussy	muttered	myrtle
must	mutterings	myself
mustache	mutton	mysterious
mustang	mutual	mysteriously
mustard	mutuality	mystery
muster	mutually	mystic
mustered	muzzle	mystical
mustiness	muzzled	mysticism
musty	my	mystification
mutability	mycology	mystify
mutable	mycosis	myth
mutate	mydriasis	mythical
mutation	mydriatic	mythological
mutative	myectomy	mythology

N

nacelle
nacre
nacreous
nadir
naiad
nail
nailed
nainsook
naïve
naïvete
naked
namable
name
named
nameless
namelessly
namely
namesake
nankeen
napery
naphtha
napkin
napoleon
Napoleonic
narcissus
narcosis
narcotic

narcotism
narcotize
narrate
narration
narrative
narrator
narrow
narrowed
narrower
narrowest
narrowly
narrowness
narwhal
nasal
nasality
nasalize
nasally
nascent
nastier
nastiest
nastily
nastiness
nasturtium
nasty
natal
natation
natatorium

nation
national
nationalism
nationalistic
nationality
nationalization
nationalize
nationally
native
nativity
natural
naturalism
naturalist
naturalistic
naturalization
naturalize
naturalized
naturally
naturalness
nature
naughtily
naughtiness
naughty
nausea
nauseate
nauseated
nauseous

nautical
nautilus
naval
navigable
navigate
navigation
navigator
navy
neap
Neapolitan
near
neared
nearer
nearest
nearly
nearness
nearsighted
neat
neater
neatest
neatly
neatness
nebula
nebular
nebulosity
nebulous
necessarily
necessary
necessitate
necessitated
necessities
necessitous
necessity
neck
neckband
neckcloth
neckerchief
necklace
necktie
neckwear
necrology
necromancy
necropolis
necropsy
necrosis
nectar
nectarine
need
needed
needful
needfully
needier
neediest
neediness
needle
needled
needless
needlework
nefarious
negation
negative
neglect
neglectful
negligence
negligent
negligible
negotiability
negotiable
negotiate
negotiated
negotiation
negotiator
Negro
negrophile
neighbor
neighborhood
neighborly
neither
nematode
Nemesis
neolithic
neon
neophyte
neoplasm
nepenthe
nephew
nepotism
nephralgia
nephrectomy
nephritis
nerve
nerveless
nervous

nescience
nest
nestle
nestled
nether
nettle
nettled
network
neural
neuralgia
neurasthenia
neurasthenic
neurectomy
neuritis
neurosis
neurotic
neutral
neutrality
neutralization
neutralize
neutralized
neutrally
never
nevermore
nevertheless
new
newcomer
newel
newer
newest
newfangled
newly
newness
newspaper
newsreel
next
nibble
niblick
nice
nicely
niceness
nicer
nicest
nicety
niche
nickel
nickeliferous
nickelodeon
nickname
nicotine
niece
niggard
niggardly
night
nightcap
nightfall
nightgown
nightingale
nightly
nightmare
nightshirt
nighttime
nightwear
nihilism
nihilist
nihilistic
nimble
nimbus
nipper
nipple
nirvana
niter
nitrate
nitric
nitride
nitrification
nitrify
nitrogen
nitrogenous
nitroglycerin
nitrous
no
nobility
noble
nobleman
nobler
noblest
nobly
nobody
nocturnal
nocturnally
nocturne
node

nodule
noel
noise
noiseless
noisier
noisiest
noisily
noisiness
noisome
noisy
nomad
nomadic
nomenclature
nominal
nominally
nominate
nominated
nomination
nominative
nominee
nonacceptance
nonadmission
nonagenarian
nonagon
nonappearance
nonattendance
nonce
nonchalance
nonchalant
nonchalantly
noncombatant

noncommissioned
noncommittal
noncommunicant
noncompliance
nonconducting
nonconductor
nonconformist
nonconformity
nonconsecutive
noncontagious
noncorrosive
nondescript
none
nonentity
nonessential
nonexistence
nonexplosive
nonfeasance
nonfeasor
nonforfeiture
nonfulfillment
noninter-
vention
nonmetallic
nonnegotiable
nonpareil
nonparticipating
nonpartisan
nonpayment
nonplus
nonprofessional
nonresidence

nonresident
nonresistance
nonresistant
nonsense
nonsensical
nonsubscriber
nonsuit
nontechnical
nonunion
nook
noon
noonday
noontime
noose
nor
norm
normal
normality
normally
Norman
Norse
north
northeast
northeaster
northeasterly
northeastern
northeastward
northerly
northern
northerner
northernmost

northland
northward
northwest
northwesterly
northwestern
Norwegian
nose
noseband
nosebleed
nosegay
nostalgia
nostril
nostrum
not
notability
notable
notarial
notary
notation
notch
note
notebook
noted
noteworthy
nothing
nothingness
notice
noticeable
notification
notify
notion

notoriety
notoriously
notwithstanding
nought
noun
nourish
nourished
nourishingly
nourishment
novaculite
novel
novelette
novelist
novelize
novelty
November
novice
novitiate
novocain
now
nowadays
nowhere
noxious
noxiousness
nozzle
nuclear
nucleate
nucleation
nucleus
nude
nudge

nudged
nudity
nugatory
nugget
nuisance
null
nullification
nullify
nullity
numb
number
numberless
numbness
numeral
numerate
numeration
numerator
numeric
numerical
numerous
numismatics
numismatist
nunnery
nuptial
nurse
nursemaid
nursery
nurseryman
nurture
nutmeg
nutrient

nutriment

nutrition

nutritious

nutritiously

nutritive

nutritively

nutshell

nuzzle

nuzzled

nyctalopia

nymph

nystagmus

O

oaf
oak
oaken
oakum
oar
oarlock
oarsman
oasis
oaten
oath
oatmeal
obbligato
obduracy
obdurate
obedience
obedient
obeisance
obelisk
obese
obesity
obey
obituary
object
objection
objectionable
objective
objectively
objectiveness
objectivity
objector
objurgate
oblate
oblation
obligate
obligation
obligatory
oblige
obliged
obligingly
oblique
obliquely
obliqueness
obliquity
obliterate
obliteration
oblivion
oblivious
obliviously
obliviousness
oblong
obloquy
obnoxious
obnoxiously
oboe
obscene
obscenity
obscure
obscured
obscureness
obscurity
obsequious
obsequiously
obsequiousness
obsequy
observable
observance
observant
observation
observatory
observe
observed
observer
observingly
obsess
obsession
obsidian
obsolescence
obsolescent
obsolete
obsoletely
obsoleteness

obstacle
obstetrical
obstetrician
obstinacy
obstinate
obstinately
obstreperous
obstruct
obstructed
obstruction
obstructionist
obstructive
obstructor
obtain
obtainable
obtrude
obtruded
obtruder
obtrusion
obtrusive
obtuse
obtusely
obtuseness
obverse
obviate
obviated
obviation
obvious
obviously
ocarina
occasion

occasional
occasionally
occident
occidental
occipital
occiput
occlude
occlusion
occult
occultation
occultism
occupancy
occupant
occupation
occupied
occupy
occur
occurred
occurrence
ocean
oceanic
oceanography
ocelot
ocher
ochlocracy
octagon
octagonal
octameter
octangular
octave
octavo

octet
October
octopus
ocular
oculist
odd
oddity
oddly
oddness
odeum
odious
odiously
odiousness
odium
odometer
odor
odoriferous
odorless
odorous
oenology
of
off
offal
offcast
offend
offense
offensive
offer
offered
offerings
offertory

offhand
office
officer
official
officially
officiate
officiated
officiation
officious
officiously
officiousness
offset
offshoot
offshore
often
oftentimes
ogee
ogive
ogle
ogled
ogre
ohm
ohmage
ohmmeter
oil
oiled
oiler
oilily
oiliness
oilskin
oilstone

oily
ointment
okra
old
olden
old-fashioned
oldish
oldness
oldster
oleaginous
oleander
oleate
oleomargarine
olfactory
oligarchy
olive
omega
omelet
omelets
omen
ominous
omission
omit
omnibus
omnipotence
omnipotent
omnipresent
omniscience
omniscient
omnivorous
on

onager
once
one
oneness
onerous
oneself
onion
onlooker
only
onomatopoeia
onslaught
onto
ontology
onus
onward
onyx
ooze
oozed
opacity
opal
opalesce
opalescence
opalescent
opaque
open
opened
opener
openings
openly
openness
openwork

opera
operable
operate
operated
operatic
operatically
operation
operative
operator
operetta
ophthalmology
opiate
opinion
opinionated
opinionative
opium
opossum
opponent
opportune
opportunity
oppose
opposed
opposite
opposition
oppress
oppression
oppressive
oppressively
oppressiveness
oppressor
opprobrious
opprobriously
opprobriousness
opprobrium
optic
optical
optician
optics
optimism
optimist
optimistic
optimistically
optimists
optimum
option
optional
optionally
optometrist
optometry
opulence
opulent
opus
or
oracle
oracular
oracularly
oral
orally
orange
orangeade
oration
orator
oratorical
oratorio
oratory
orb
orbit
orchard
orchestra
orchestral
orchestrate
orchestrated
orchestration
orchid
orchidaceous
ordain
ordained
ordeal
orderliness
orderly
ordinal
ordinance
ordinarily
ordinary
ordination
ordnance
organ
organic
organically
organism
organist
organization
organize

orgy
orient
oriental
orientalism
orientalist
orientate
orientation
orifice
origin
original
originality
originally
originate
originated
origination
originative
originator
oriole
Orion
orlop
ormolu
ornament
ornamental
ornamentally
ornamentation
ornate
ornithological
ornithologist
ornithology
orotund
orphan
orphanage
orphanhood
orrery
orthodox
orthoëpy
orthography
orthopedic
ortolan
oscillate
oscillated
oscillation
oscillator
oscillatory
osculate
osculation
osculatory
osier
osmium
osmosis
osprey
osseous
ossification
ossify
ostensible
ostensibly
ostentation
ostentatious
ostentatiously
osteopath
osteopathy
ostracism
ostracize
ostracized
ostrich
otalgia
other
otherwise
otiose
otitis
otorrhea
otter
ottoman
ought
ounce
our
ours
ourselves
oust
ouster
out
outcast
outclass
outcome
outcrop
outcroppings
outcry
outcurve
outdistance
outdo
outdoors
outer
outermost

outfield
outfit
outfitter
outflank
outgo
outgrowth
outings
outlandish
outlandishness
outlast
outlaw
outlay
outlet
outlets
outline
outlive
outlook
outmarch
outnumber
outrage
outraged
outrageous
outrageously
outrageousness
outrank
outreach
outrider
outrigger
outright
outrun
outset

outside
outsider
outsize
outskirt
outstandingly
outstay
outstrip
outtalk
outward
outwardly
outwear
outwit
oval
ovation
oven
over
overalls
overanxious
overawe
overbalance
overbear
overbid
overboard
overburden
overcapitalize
overcast
overcautious
overcharge
overclothes
overcoat
overcome

overconfident
overdevelop
overdo
overdose
overdraft
overdress
overdriven
overdue
overestimate
overexpose
overexposure
overflow
overgrown
overhand
overhang
overhaul
overhead
overheat
overindulge
overindulgence
overissue
overlap
overload
overlook
overlord
overmaster
overnight
overpay
overpowered
overpoweringly
overproduction

overrate
overrated
overreach
override
overripe
overrule
overrun
overseas
overseer
overshadow
overshadowed
overshoe
oversight
oversize
overspread
overstate
overstatement
overstep
overstock

overstrain
oversubscribe
oversupply
overt
overtake
overthrow
overtime
overtone
overture
overturn
overturned
overvalue
overweight
overwhelm
overwhelmed
overwhelmingly
overwork
overwrought
ovum

owe
owed
owl
owlet
owlets
owlish
own
owned
owner
ownership
oxalate
oxalic
oxidation
oxide
oxidize
oxygen
oxyhydrogen
oyster
ozone

P

pabulum
pace
pacemaker
pacer
pachyderm
pacific
pacification
pacifier
pacifism
pacifist
pacify
pack
package
packer
packet
packings
packsaddle
pact
pad
paddle
paddled
paddock
padlock
pagan
paganism
page
pageant
pageantry
pagination
pagoda
paid
pail
pain
painful
painless
painstaking
paint
painted
painter
pair
paired
pairings
pajama
palace
palanquin
palatability
palatable
palate
palatial
palatially
palatinate
pale
paleography
palette
palfrey
palimpsest
palindrome
palings
palisade
pall
palladium
pallbearer
palliate
palliated
palliation
palliative
pallid
pallium
pallor
palm
palmetto
palmist
palmistry
palpability
palpable
palpate
palpation
palpitant
palpitate
palpitatingly
palpitation

palsied
palsy
paltry
pampas
pamper
pamphlet
pamphlets
panacea
pancake
panchromatic
pancreas
pancreatic
panda
pandemic
pandemonium
pander
pandered
panegyric
panegyrical
panegyrize
panel
paneled
pang
panic
pannier
pannikin
panorama
panoramic
pansy
pant
pantaloon

pantheon
panther
pantograph
pantomime
pantry
papacy
papal
paper
papered
papeterie
papoose
paprika
parable
parabola
parabolic
parabolical
parachute
parade
paradigm
paradise
paradox
paradoxical
paraffin
paragon
paragraph
parallax
parallel
paralleled
parallelogram
paralysis
paralytic

paralyze
paralyzed
paramount
paranoia
paranoiac
parapet
paraphernalia
paraphrase
paraplegia
paraplegic
parasite
parasitic
parasitical
parasiticide
parasol
parboil
parcel
parceled
parch
parchment
pardon
pardonable
pardoned
pare
pared
paregoric
parent
parentage
parental
parentheses
parenthesis

parenthetical
parenthetically
parenthood
parietal
parings
parish
parishioner
parity
park
parka
parkway
parlance
parley
parliament
parliamentarian
parliamentary
parlor
parochial
parody
parole
paroxysm
paroxysmal
parquet
parricidal
parricide
parrot
parry
parse
parsimonious
parsimony
parsley

parsnip
parsonage
part
partake
parted
parterre
partial
partiality
partially
participant
participate
participated
participation
participator
participial
participle
particle
particular
particularity
particularize
particularized
particularly
partisan
partisanship
partition
partitioned
partner
partnership
partridge
party
parvenu

paschal
pass
passable
passage
passageway
passbook
passed
passenger
passion
passionate
passionately
passionless
passive
passivity
passover
passport
password
past
paste
pasteboard
pastel
pastern
pasteurized
pastime
pastor
pastoral
pastorate
pastrami
pastry
pasturage
patch

patchwork
patchy
patella
patellar
patent
patentable
patented
patentee
paternal
paternalism
paternally
paternity
path
pathetic
pathless
pathologist
pathology
pathos
pathway
patience
patient
patina
patio
patness
patriarch
patriarchal
patriarchate
patrician
patrimonial
patrimony
patriot
patriotic
patriotically
patriotism
patrol
patrolled
patrolman
patron
patronage
patroness
patronize
patronized
patronymic
patter
pattered
pattern
patterned
paucity
Paulist
pauper
pauperism
pauperization
pauperize
pause
paused
pave
paved
pavement
pavilion
paw
pawl
pawn
pawnbroker
pawned
pawnshop
pay
payable
payee
payer
paymaster
payment
pea
peace
peaceable
peaceably
peaceful
peacemaker
peach
peacock
peak
peaked
peal
pealed
peanut
pear
pearl
pearlite
pearly
peasant
peasantry
peat
peavey
pebble

pebbled
pebbly
pecan
peccadillo
peccancy
peccant
peccary
peck
pectase
pectin
pectoral
peculate
peculiar
peculiarity
peculiarly
pecuniary
pedagogic
pedagogical
pedagogue
pedagogy
pedal
pedant
pedantic
pedantical
pedantry
peddle
peddler
pedestal
pedestrian
pedestrianism
pediatrician
pediatrics
pedicular
pediculosis
pedigree
pedigreed
pediment
pedometer
peek
peel
peeled
peelings
peep
peer
peerage
peered
peeress
peerless
peevish
peg
Pegasus
pelagic
pelf
pelican
pelisse
pellagra
pellet
pellets
pellucid
pelota
pelt
pelted
peltry
pelvic
pelvis
pemmican
pen
penal
penalization
penalize
penalized
penalty
penance
penchant
pencil
penciled
pendant
pendency
pending
pendulous
pendulum
penetrability
penetrable
penetrant
penetrate
penetration
penetrative
penguin
penholder
penicillin
penicillium
peninsula
peninsular

penitence
penitent
penitential
penitentiary
penitently
penknife
penman
penmanship
pennant
penniless
penny
penologist
penology
pension
pensionary
pensioner
pensive
penstock
pent
pentagon
pentameter
Pentateuch
pentathlon
Pentecost
penthouse
penult
penultimate
penumbra
penurious
penury
peon

peony
people
peplum
pepper
pepperiness
peppermint
peppery
pepsin
peptic
peradventure
perambulate
perambulator
perborate
percale
perceivable
perceive
per cent
percentage
percentile
perceptibility
perceptible
perception
perceptive
perceptual
perch
perchance
percipiency
percipient
percolate
percolation
percolator

percussion
percussive
peregrination
peremptorily
peremptoriness
peremptory
perennial
perfect
perfectibility
perfectible
perfection
perfectly
perfidious
perfidy
perforate
perforation
perforator
perforce
perform
performable
performance
performed
performer
perfume
perfumed
perfumer
perfumery
perfunctory
pergola
perhaps
peril

perilous	permeation	persecutor
perilously	permissibility	perseverance
perimeter	permissible	persevere
period	permission	persevered
periodate	permissive	persiflage
periodic	permit	persimmon
periodical	permitted	persist
periodicity	permutation	persistence
peripatetic	permutite	persistency
peripheral	pernicious	persistent
periphery	peroration	persists
periphrastic	peroxide	person
periscope	perpendicular	personable
perish	perpetrate	personage
perishable	perpetration	personal
peristyle	perpetrator	personality
peritoneum	perpetual	personalize
peritonitis	perpetually	personally
periwinkle	perpetuate	personalty
perjure	perpetuated	personification
perjured	perpetuation	personify
perjurer	perpetuator	personnel
perjury	perpetuity	perspective
permanence	perplex	perspicacious
permanent	perplexed	perspicacity
permanently	perplexedly	perspicuous
permanganate	perplexingly	perspiration
permeability	perplexity	perspiratory
permeable	perquisite	perspire
permeate	persecute	perspired
permeated	persecution	persuade

persuaded
persuader
persuasion
persuasive
persuasiveness
persulphate
pert
pertain
pertinacious
pertinacity
pertinence
pertinency
pertinent
perturb
perturbable
perturbation
perusal
peruse
perused
Peruvian
pervade
pervasion
pervasive
perverse
perversion
perversity
perversive
pervert
perverted
pervious
pessimism

pessimist
pessimistic
pessimists
pester
pesthouse
pestiferous
pestilence
pestilent
pestilential
pestle
pet
petal
petaliferous
petard
petite
petition
petitioner
petrel
petrifaction
petrifactive
petrify
petrol
petrolatum
petroleum
petrology
petticoat
pettily
pettiness
pettish
petty
petulance

petulant
petunia
pew
pewter
phaeton
phalanges
phalanx
phantasm
phantom
pharmaceutic
pharmaceutical
pharmacist
pharmacology
pharmacopoeia
pharmacy
pharyngitis
pharynx
phase
pheasant
phenol
phenomena
phenomenal
phenomenology
phenomenon
phial
philander
philanderer
philanthropic
philanthropical
philanthropist
philanthropy

philately
philatelic
philatelist
philharmonic
philippic
Philippine
Philistine
philologist
philology
philosopher
philosophic
philosophical
philosophize
philosophy
philter
phlebitis
phlebotomy
phlegm
phlegmatic
phlox
phobia
phone
phonetic
phonetician
phonetics
phonic
phonograph
phosphate
phosphide
phosphite
phosphoresce

phosphorescence
phosphorescent
phosphoric
phosphorus
photoelectric
photoengraving
photogenic
photograph
photographer
photographic
photography
photogravure
photolithograph
photomicrograph
photoplay
photostat
phrase
phrased
phraseology
phrenetic
phrenic
phrenologist
phrenology
phthisis
phylactery
physic
physical
physically
physician
physics
physiognomy

physiology
physique
pianist
piano
piazza
pica
picaresque
piccolo
pick
pickax
picker
pickerel
picket
pickle
picklock
pickpocket
pickup
picnic
picnicker
picric
pictograph
pictorial
pictorially
picture
pictured
picturesque
pie
piece
piecemeal
piecework
pied

pieplant
pier
pierce
pierced
piety
pig
pigeon
pigeonhole
piggery
piggish
pigheaded
pigment
pigmentation
pigmy
pigskin
pigsty
pigtail
pigwood
pike
piker
pikestaff
pilaster
pilchard
pile
piled
pilfer
pilgrim
pilgrimage
pillage
pillar
pillion

pillory
pillow
pillowcase
pilot
pimento
pimple
pin
pinafore
pincers
pinch
pincushion
pine
pineapple
pinfeather
pinfish
ping-pong
pinguid
pinhole
pinion
pink
pinnace
pinnacle
pinochle
pinto
pinweed
pioneer
pioneered
pious
piously
pip
pipage

pipe
pipette
piquancy
piquant
pique
piracy
piragua
pirate
pirated
piratic
piratical
pirogue
pirouette
piscatology
piscatorial
pistachio
pistol
piston
pit
pitch
pitcher
piteous
piteousness
pitfall
pith
pithily
pithiness
pithy
pitiable
pitiful
pitiless

pitilessly
pitilessness
pittance
pitted
pituitary
pity
pityingly
pivot
pivotal
placability
placable
placard
placate
placated
placatory
place
placebo
placeman
placement
placer
placid
placidity
placidly
placket
plagiarism
plagiarist
plagiarize
plagiary
plague
plaid
plain
plainly
plainness
plaint
plaintiff
plaintive
plan
planchette
plane
planet
planetaria
planetarium
planetary
planetoid
plangent
plank
planked
plankton
planned
plant
plantain
plantation
planted
planter
plantings
plasma
plaster
plastered
plasterer
plastic
plasticity
plate
plateau
plated
plateful
platen
plater
platform
platina
platinate
platinic
platiniferous
platinoid
platinum
platitude
platitudinize
platitudinous
platoon
platter
platypus
plaudit
plausibility
plausible
play
player
playful
playfulness
playgoer
playground
playings
playmate
plaything
playtime

playwright
plaza
plea
plead
pleader
pleadingly
pleadings
pleasant
pleasantly
pleasantness
pleasantry
please
pleasurable
pleasure
plebeian
plebiscite
plectrum
pledge
pledgee
pledger
pledget
pledgor
plenary
plenarily
plenipotentiary
plenitude
plenteous
plentiful
plenty
plenum
pleonasm

pleonastic
plethora
plethoric
pleura
pleurisy
plexus
pliability
pliable
pliably
pliancy
pliant
plier
pliers
plight
plinth
plodder
plot
plotted
plotter
plough
plover
plow
plowboy
plowman
plowshare
pluck
pluckily
plucky
plug
plugged
plum

plumage
plumb
plumbago
plumbate
plumber
plumbic
plumbous
plume
plumed
plummet
plump
plumper
plumpest
plumply
plumpness
plunder
plundered
plunderer
plunge
plunged
plunger
plunk
plural
plurality
pluralize
plus
plush
plutocracy
plutocrat
plutocratic
plutonic

pluvial
ply
pneumatic
pneumatically
pneumatics
pneumonia
poach
poacher
pocket
pocketbook
pocketknife
pockmark
pod
podagra
podiatry
poem
poet
poetaster
poetic
poetical
poetry
poignancy
poignant
poinciana
poinsettia
point
pointed
pointedly
pointer
pointless
pointlessly

poise
poised
poison
poisoned
poisoner
poisonous
poke
poker
pokeweed
polar
polarity
polarization
polarize
polarized
polarizer
pole
polecat
polemic
polemical
polemicist
police
policeman
policy
polish
polisher
polite
politely
politeness
politic
political
politically

politician
politicly
politics
polity
polka
poll
pollen
pollinate
pollination
polliniferous
pollute
polluted
pollution
polo
polonaise
polonium
poltroon
polyandrous
polyandry
polychrome
polyclinic
polygamist
polygamous
polygamy
polyglot
polygon
polygonal
polymeric
polyp
polyphony
polysyllabic

polytechnic
pomade
pommel
pomology
pomp
pompadour
pompano
pomposity
pompous
poncho
pond
ponder
ponderable
pondered
ponderous
pondweed
pongee
poniard
pontiff
pontifically
pontificate
pontoon
pony
poodle
pool
pooled
poor
poorer
poorest
poorhouse
poorly

poorness
popcorn
poplar
poplin
poppet
poppy
populace
popular
popularity
popularization
popularize
popularized
popularly
populate
populated
population
populous
porcelain
porch
porcupine
pore
pork
pornography
porosity
porous
porphyry
porpoise
porringer
port
portable
portage

portal
portcullis
portend
portent
portentous
porter
porterhouse
portfolio
porthole
portico
portiere
portion
portrait
portraiture
portray
portrayal
Portuguese
portulaca
pose
poses
position
positive
posse
possess
possession
possessive
possessor
possessorship
possibility
possible
possum

post
postage
postal
postdate
postdated
poster
posterior
posterity
postern
postgraduate
posthaste
posthumous
postilion
postlude
postman
postmark
postmaster
postoperative
postpaid
postpone
postponed
postponement
postprandial
postscript
postulant
postulate
postulation
posture
postured
posturings
posy
pot
potable
potash
potassium
potation
potato
potboiler
potency
potent
potentate
potential
potentiality
potentially
pothole
pothook
potion
potlatch
potluck
potpie
potpourri
potsherd
pottage
potter
pottery
pouch
poultice
poultry
pounce
pound
poundage
poundcake
poundings
pour
pout
poverty
powder
powdered
powdery
power
powerful
powerfully
powerless
powerlessly
powerlessness
powwow
practicability
practicable
practicably
practical
practicality
practically
practice
practitioner
pragmatic
pragmatism
pragmatist
prairie
praise
praised
praiseworthy
praline
prance

prank
prate
pratique
prattle
prawn
pray
prayer
prayerful
prayerfully
preach
preacher
preachment
preamble
prearrange
prearrangement
prebendary
precanceled
precarious
precaution
precautionary
precede
preceded
precedence
precedent
precept
preceptor
preceptress
precinct
precious
preciously
precipice
precipitancy
precipitant
precipitate
precipitately
precipitation
precipitous
precise
precision
preclude
preclusion
precocious
precociously
precocity
preconceived
preconception
precursor
precursory
predaceous
predacity
predatory
predecease
predecessor
predestination
predestine
predeterminate
predetermine
prediastolic
predicament
predicate
predicated
predication
predict
predictable
prediction
predictive
predigest
predigestion
predilection
predispose
predisposed
predisposition
predominant
predominate
pre-eminence
pre-eminent
pre-empt
pre-emption
preen
preface
prefaced
prefatory
prefect
prefer
preferable
preferably
preference
preferential
preferentially
preferment
preferred
prefix
preform

pregnancy
pregnant
prehensile
prehistoric
prejudge
prejudice
prejudiced
prejudicial
prejudicially
prelate
preliminary
prelude
premature
premeditate
premeditated
premeditation
premier
premise
premises
premium
premonition
premonitory
prenatal
preoccupation
preoccupied
preoccupy
prepaid
preparation
preparative
preparatory
prepare

prepared
preparedness
prepay
prepayment
preponderance
preponderant
preponderate
preponderatingly
preposition
prepositional
prepossess
prepossession
preposterous
prerequisite
prerogative
presage
presbyter
presbyterian
presbytery
prescience
prescient
prescribe
prescribed
prescription
prescriptive
presence
present
presentability
presentable
presentation
presentiment

presently
presentment
preservation
preservative
preserve
preserver
preside
presidency
president
presidential
press
pressboard
pressman
pressure
presswork
prestidigitator
prestige
presto
presumable
presumably
presume
presumed
presumedly
presumption
presumptive
presumptuous
presuppose
presystolic
pretend
pretended
pretender

pretense
pretension
pretensions
pretentious
preterit
preternatural
pretext
pretexts
prettier
prettiest
prettily
prettiness
pretty
pretzel
prevail
prevailed
prevalence
prevalent
prevalently
prevaricate
prevarication
prevaricator
prevent
preventability
preventable
prevented
prevention
preventive
preview
previous
prevision

prey
price
priced
prices
priceless
prick
prickle
prickliness
prickly
pride
prideful
priest
priestess
priesthood
priestly
priggish
prim
primacy
primal
primarily
primary
primate
primateship
prime
primed
primer
primer
primeval
primitive
primly
primness

primogeniture
primordial
primrose
prince
princeliness
princely
princes
princess
principal
principality
principally
principle
print
printable
printed
printer
printery
printings
prior
priority
priory
prism
prismatic
prison
prisoner
pristine
privacy
private
privateer
privately
privateness

privation
privet
privilege
privily
privity
privy
prize
prized
probability
probable
probably
probate
probation
probationary
probe
probity
problem
problematic
proboscis
procedural
procedure
proceed
proceeded
proceedings
process
processed
processes
procession
processional
proclaim
proclaimed

proclamation
proclivity
proconsul
procrastinate
procrastination
procrastinator
proctor
procurable
procuration
procurator
procure
procured
procurement
prodigal
prodigality
prodigious
prodigiously
prodigy
produce
produced
producer
produces
product
production
productive
productivity
proem
profanation
profanatory
profane
profanity

profess
professed
professedly
profession
professional
professionalism
professionally
professor
professorial
professorship
proffer
proficiency
proficient
proficiently
profile
profit
profitable
profitably
profiteer
profitless
profligacy
profligate
profound
profoundness
profundity
profuse
profusely
profuseness
profusion
progenitor
progeny

prognosis
prognostic
prognosticate
prognostication
program
progress
progression
progressive
prohibit
prohibition
prohibitionist
prohibitory
project
projectile
projection
projector
proletarian
proletariat
proliferate
proliferation
prolific
prolix
prolixity
prologue
prolong
prolongate
prolongation
prolonged
promenade
prominence
prominent
promiscuity
promiscuous
promiscuously
promiscuousness
promise
promisingly
promissory
promontory
promote
promoted
promoter
promotion
prompt
prompted
prompter
promptitude
promptly
promptness
promulgate
promulgation
pronate
pronation
prone
prong
pronghorn
pronominal
pronoun
pronounce
pronounceable
pronounced
pronouncement
pronunciation
proof
prop
propaganda
propagandist
propagate
propagated
propagation
propane
propel
propellant
propelled
propeller
propensity
proper
properly
properties
property
prophecy
prophesied
prophesy
prophet
prophetic
prophetically
prophylactic
prophylaxis
propinquity
propitiate
propitiated
propitiation
propitiatory

propitious
proponent
proportion
proportionable
proportional
proportionally
proportionate
proportionately
proposal
propose
proposed
proposition
propound
proprietary
proprietor
propriety
proptosis
propulsion
prorate
prorogation
prorogue
prorogued
prosaic
proscenium
proscribe
proscribed
proscription
prose
prosecute
prosecuted
prosecution

prosecutor
proselyte
proselytize
prosily
prosiness
prosody
prospect
prospective
prospector
prospectus
prosper
prosperity
prosperous
prosperously
prosthesis
prosthetic
prostrate
prostration
prosy
protagonist
protagonists
protean
protect
protected
protectingly
protection
protectionist
protective
protectively
protectiveness
protector

protectorate
protein
protest
protestant
protestation
protestingly
protests
prothonotary
protocol
protoplasm
prototype
protoxide
protozoa
protract
protraction
protractive
protractor
protrude
protruded
protrusion
protrusive
protuberance
protuberant
proud
prouder
proudest
proudly
provable
prove
provender
proverb

proverbial
provide
provided
providence
provident
providential
providentially
provider
province
provincial
provincialism
provinciality
provincially
provision
provisional
proviso
provisory
provocation
provocative
provoke
provokingly
provost
prow
prowess
prowl
proximal
proximate
proximity
proximo
proxy
prude
prudence
prudent
prudential
prudentially
prudently
prudery
prudish
prune
pruned
prurience
prurient
Prussian
pry
pryingly
psalm
psalmist
Psalter
pseudonym
psoriasis
psychiatric
psychiatrist
psychiatry
psychic
psychical
psychoanalysis
psychological
psychologist
psychology
psychopathic
psychopathology
psychosis
ptomaine
public
publication
publicist
publicity
publicly
publish
publisher
puce
puck
pucker
pudding
puddle
puddled
puddler
pudency
pudginess
pudgy
pueblo
puerile
puerility
puff
puffin
puffiness
puffy
pug
pugilism
pugilist
pugilistic
pugnacious
pugnaciously

pugnacity
puissance
puissant
pull
pulled
pullet
pulley
Pullman
pullulate
pulmonary
pulmotor
pulp
pulpiness
pulpit
pulpiteer
pulpy
pulsate
pulsated
pulsation
pulsator
pulsatory
pulse
pulverization
pulverize
pulverizer
pumice
pump
pumpernickel
pumpkin
pun
punch

puncheon
punctilio
punctilious
punctiliously
punctiliousness
punctual
punctuality
punctually
punctuate
punctuated
punctuation
puncture
punctured
pung
pungency
pungent
puniness
punish
punishable
punishment
punitive
punk
puny
pup
pupa
pupae
pupil
puppet
puppetry
puppy
purblind

purchasable
purchase
purchased
purchaser
pure
purely
purer
purest
purgative
purgatory
purge
purification
purifier
purify
purism
purist
puritan
puritanic
puritanical
Puritanism
purity
purl
purlieu
purloin
purple
purplish
purport
purported
purpose
purposeful
purposeless

purposely	push	puzzle
purr	pushcart	puzzled
purse	pusher	puzzler
purser	pusillanimous	pyelitis
purslane	pustulant	pyemia
pursuance	pustular	pygmy
pursuant	pustulate	pylon
pursue	pustulation	pylorus
pursued	pustule	pyonephrosis
pursuit	put	pyorrhea
pursuivant	putative	pyramid
pursy	putrefaction	pyramidal
purulence	putrefactive	pyre
purulency	putrefy	pyrexia
purulent	putrescence	pyrites
purvey	putrescent	pyrography
purveyance	putrid	pyrometer
purveyor	putt	pyrotechnics
purview	putter	pyroxylin
pus	putty	python

Q

quack
quackery
quadrangle
quadratic
quadratics
quadrature
quadrennial
quadrennially
quadrilateral
quadrille
quadruped
quadruple
quadruplex
quadruplicate
quaff
quagmire
quahog
quail
quailed
quaint
quaintly
quaintness
Quaker
qualification
qualified
qualify
qualitative
qualities
quality
qualm
quandary
quantitative
quantities
quantity
quantum
quarantine
quarrel
quarreled
quarrelsome
quarry
quart
quartan
quarter
quartered
quarterly
quartermaster
quartet
quartile
quarto
quartz
quash
quasi
quaternary
quatrain
quaver
quavered
quay
quayage
queen
queenly
queer
quell
quelled
quench
quenchless
querulous
query
quest
question
questionable
questioner
questionnaire
queue
quibble
quick
quicken
quickened
quicklime
quickly
quickness
quicksand

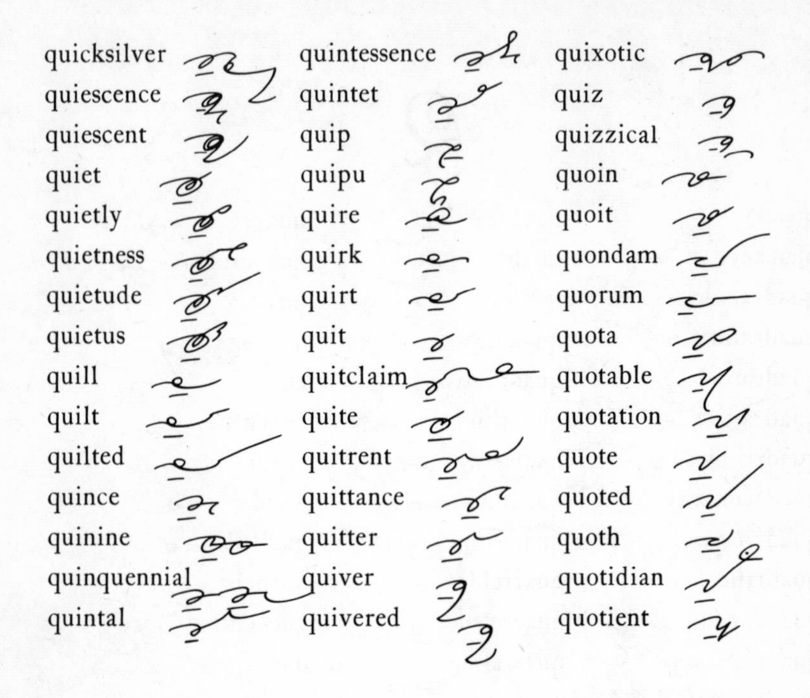

quicksilver
quiescence
quiescent
quiet
quietly
quietness
quietude
quietus
quill
quilt
quilted
quince
quinine
quinquennial
quintal
quintessence
quintet
quip
quipu
quire
quirk
quirt
quit
quitclaim
quite
quitrent
quittance
quitter
quiver
quivered
quixotic
quiz
quizzical
quoin
quoit
quondam
quorum
quota
quotable
quotation
quote
quoted
quoth
quotidian
quotient

R

rabbet
rabbinical
rabbit
rabbitry
rabble
rabid
rabidly
rabies
raccoon
race
raced
racer
raceway
rachitic
rachitis
racial
racially
racily
raciness
rack
racket
raconteur
radial
radially
radiance
radiancy
radiant

radiantly
radiate
radiated
radiation
radiator
radical
radicalism
radically
radii
radio
radiogram
radiophone
radish
radium
radius
radiuses
radon
raffia
raffle
raffled
raft
rafter
raftsman
rag
ragamuffin
rage
ragged

raglan
ragout
ragpicker
ragtime
ragweed
raid
rail
railed
railhead
railings
raillery
railroad
railway
raiment
rain
rainbow
raincoat
rainfall
rainstorm
rainy
raise
raisin
rajah
rake
rakish
rally
ram

ramble
rambled
rambler
ramekin
ramification
ramify
rammed
ramp
rampage
rampant
rampart
ramrod
ramshackle
ranch
rancher
ranchman
rancho
rancid
rancidity
rancidly
rancor
rancorous
random
range
ranger
rank
ranked
rankle
ransack
ransom
rant

rantingly
rapacious
rapaciously
rapacity
rapid
rapidity
rapidly
rapier
rapine
rapport
rapt
raptorial
rapture
rapturous
rapturously
rapturousness
rarefaction
rarefy
rarely
rareness
rarity
rascal
rascality
rascally
rash
rasher
rashest
rashly
rashness
rasp
raspberry

rat
ratchet
rate
rated
rather
rathskeller
ratification
ratify
ratings
ratio
ratiocination
ratiocinative
ration
rational
rationalism
rationalistic
rationalization
rationalize
rationalized
rationally
rationed
ratline
rattan
ratter
rattle
rattled
rattler
rattlesnake
rattly
raucous
ravage

ravaged
rave
ravel
raveled
raven
ravenous
ravine
ravish
ravished
ravishment
raw
rawboned
rawhide
rawness
ray
rayless
rayon
raze
razed
razor
razorback
reach
react
reaction
reactionary
read
readability
readable
reader
readily
readiness

readings
readjust
readjustment
readmission
readmit
ready
reaffirm
reaffirmation
reagent
real
realism
realist
realistic
realistically
reality
realizable
realization
realize
realized
really
realm
realtor
realty
ream
reamer
reanimate
reap
reaper
reappear
reappearance
reappoint

reappointment
rear
reared
reargue
rearm
rearmament
rearmed
rearmost
rearrange
rearrangement
rearward
reason
reasonable
reasonableness
reasonably
reassemble
reassert
reasserted
reassign
reassigned
reassume
reassumed
reassurance
reassure
reassured
rebate
rebated
rebel
rebellion
rebellious
rebind

rebirth
reborn
rebound
rebuff
rebuild
rebuilt
rebuke
rebukingly
rebus
rebut
rebuttal
rebutter
recalcitrant
recall
recalled
recant
recanted
recapitalization
recapitalize
recapitulate
recapitulated
recapitulation
recapture
recast
recede
receded
receipt
receipted
receivable
receive
received

receiver
receivership
recent
recently
receptacle
receptive
receptively
receptiveness
receptivity
recess
recesses
recession
recessional
recessive
recharge
recidivism
recipe
recipient
reciprocal
reciprocally
reciprocate
reciprocation
reciprocative
reciprocator
reciprocity
recital
recitalist
recitation
recitative
recite
recited

reck
reckless
reckon
reckoned
reckoner
reclaim
reclaimable
reclaimed
reclamation
recline
reclined
recluse
recognition
recognizable
recognizance
recognize
recognized
recoil
recoiled
recollect
recollected
recollection
recommence
recommend
recommendation
recommendatory
recommended
recommit
recompense
reconcilable
reconcile

reconciled
reconcilement
reconciliation
reconciliatory
recondite
reconnaissance
reconnoiter
reconnoitered
reconquer
reconquered
reconsider
reconstitute
reconstruct
reconstruction
reconstructive
record
recorded
recorder
recordings
recount
recounted
recoup
recoupment
recourse
recover
recoverable
recovery
recreant
recreation
recriminate
recrimination

recriminative
recriminatory
recrudescence
recrudescent
recruit
recruitment
recrystallize
rectal
rectangle
rectangular
rectification
rectifier
rectify
rectilinear
rectitude
rector
rectory
recumbency
recumbent
recuperate
recuperated
recuperation
recuperative
recuperatory
recur
recurred
recurrence
recurrent
recusant
red
redbreast

redden
redder
reddest
reddish
redeem
redeemed
redeemer
redemption
redemptory
redirect
redirected
rediscount
rediscover
redistribute
redistribution
redness
redolence
redolent
redouble
redoubt
redoubtable
redound
redress
reduce
reduced
reducer
reducible
reduction
redundance
redundancy
redundant

re-echo
reed
reediness
reedy
reef
reefer
reel
re-elect
re-embark
re-embarkation
re-enact
re-enforce
re-enforcement
re-engage
re-engrave
re-enlist
re-enter
re-entry
re-establish
re-examination
re-examine
re-export
re-exportation
refectory
refer
referable
referee
reference
referendum
referred
refine

refined
refinement
refiner
refinery
refit
reflect
reflected
reflection
reflective
reflector
reflex
reflexes
reflexive
reforestation
reform
reformation
reformative
reformatory
reformed
reformer
refract
refracted
refraction
refractive
refractivity
refractor
refractory
refrain
refrained
refresh
refresher

refreshingly
refreshment
refrigerant
refrigerate
refrigerated
refrigeration
refrigerative
refrigerator
refuge
refugee
refulgence
refulgent
refund
refunded
refurnish
refusal
refuse
refused
refuses
refutation
refute
refuted
regain
regained
regal
regale
regaled
regalement
regalia
regally
regard

regardful
regardless
regards
regatta
regency
regeneracy
regenerate
regeneration
regenerative
regenerator
regent
regicide
regimen
regiment
regimental
regimentals
regimentation
region
regional
regionally
register
registered
registrar
registration
registry
regress
regression
regressive
regret
regretful
regretfully
regretfulness
regrettable
regretted
regular
regularity
regularly
regulate
regulated
regulates
regulation
regulator
regurgitate
regurgitation
rehabilitate
rehabilitation
rehearsal
rehearse
reign
reimburse
reimbursed
reimbursement
reimport
reimportation
rein
reincarnate
reincarnation
reindeer
reinsert
reinstall
reinstate
reinsurance
reinsure
reintroduce
reinvest
reinvigorate
reinvigoration
reissue
reiterate
reiteration
reiterative
reject
rejected
rejection
rejoice
rejoiced
rejoices
rejoin
rejoinder
rejuvenate
rejuvenation
rejuvenescent
rekindle
relapse
relapsed
relate
related
relation
relational
relationship
relative
relatively
relativity

relator
relax
relaxation
relaxed
relaxes
relay
release
released
relegate
relegated
relegation
relent
relented
relentless
relevance
relevancy
relevant
reliability
reliable
reliance
reliant
relic
relief
relievable
relieve
religion
religious
religiously
relinquish
relinquishment
reliquary

relish
relive
reload
relucent
reluctance
reluctant
reluctantly
rely
remain
remainder
remained
remake
remand
remark
remarkable
remarry
remediable
remedial
remedied
remedy
remember
remembered
remembrance
remind
reminder
remindful
reminiscence
reminiscent
remiss
remission
remit

remittal
remittance
remitted
remittent
remitter
remnant
remodel
remonetize
remonstrance
remonstrant
remonstrate
remonstrated
remonstration
remonstrative
remorse
remorseful
remorsefully
remorseless
remote
remoteness
remount
removability
removable
removal
remove
remunerate
remuneration
remunerative
renaissance
renal
render

rendered
rendezvous
rendition
renegade
renew
renewable
renewal
renewed
rennet
renominate
renominated
renounce
renovate
renovated
renovation
renown
renowned
rent
rental
rented
renumber
renunciation
renunciatory
reopen
reorder
reorganization
reorganize
reorient
repaid
repair
repaired

reparable
reparation
reparative
repartee
repast
repatriate
repay
repayment
repeal
repealed
repeat
repeatedly
repeater
repel
repelled
repellence
repellent
repent
repentance
repentant
repented
repercussion
repercussive
repertoire
repertory
repetition
repetitious
repetitive
rephrase
repine
repined

replace
replaced
replacement
replant
replenish
replenishment
replete
repletion
replevin
replica
replied
reply
report
reported
reporter
repose
reposed
reposeful
repository
repossess
repossessed
reprehend
reprehensible
reprehension
reprehensive
represent
representation
representative
repress
repression
repressive

reprieve
reprimand
reprimandingly
reprint
reprinted
reprisal
reproach
reproachful
reproachfully
reproachfulness
reprobate
reprobation
reproduce
reproducer
reproduction
reproductive
reproof
reprove
reproved
reprovingly
reptile
reptilian
republic
republican
republicanism
republicanize
republish
repudiate
repudiated
repudiation
repugnance
repugnant
repulse
repulsed
repulsion
repulsive
repurchase
reputable
reputation
repute
reputed
reputedly
request
requests
requiem
require
requirement
requires
requisite
requisition
requital
requite
reredos
rerun
resale
rescind
rescinded
rescript
rescue
rescued
research
resection
resemblance
resemble
resent
resented
resentful
resentfully
resentfulness
resentment
reservation
reserve
reserved
reservist
reservoir
resettle
resettlement
reship
reshipment
reside
residence
residency
resident
residential
residual
residuary
residue
residuum
resign
resignation
resigned
resignedly
resiliency

resilient
resin
resist
resistance
resistant
resistible
resistivity
resistless
resists
resoluble
resolute
resoluteness
resolution
resolvable
resolve
resolved
resolvent
resonance
resonant
resonate
resonator
resort
resorted
resound
resounded
resoundingly
resource
resourceful
resourcefulness
respect
respectability

respectable
respected
respecter
respective
respects
respirable
respiration
respirator
respiratory
respire
respite
resplendence
resplendency
resplendent
respond
responded
respondent
response
responsibility
responsible
responsive
rest
restate
restatement
restaurant
restaurateur
rested
restful
restfully
restfulness
restitution

restive
restively
restiveness
restless
restock
restoration
restorative
restore
restored
restrain
restrained
restrainingly
restraint
restrict
restricted
restriction
restrictive
rests
result
resultant
resumable
resume
resumed
resumption
resurface
resurgence
resurgent
resurrect
resurrected
resurrection
resuscitate

resuscitated
resuscitation
resuscitative
retail
retailed
retailer
retain
retained
retainer
retake
retaliate
retaliated
retaliation
retaliative
retaliatory
retard
retardation
retarded
retch
retell
retention
retentive
retentivity
reticence
reticent
reticle
reticular
reticulate
reticule
retina
retinal

retinitis
retinue
retire
retired
retirement
retold
retort
retorted
retouch
retoucher
retrace
retraceable
retract
retracted
retractile
retraction
retractive
retractor
retread
retreat
retreated
retrench
retrenchment
retrial
retribution
retributive
retrievable
retrieve
retrieved
retriever
retroactive

retroactivity
retrocession
retrograde
retrogression
retrogressive
retrospect
retrospection
retrospective
retroversion
return
returnable
reunion
reunite
revalue
revamp
reveal
revealed
revealingly
revealment
reveille
revel
revelation
reveler
revelry
revenge
revenged
revengeful
revenue
reverberant
reverberate
reverberation

reverberative
reverberator
reverberatory
revere
revered
reverence
reverend
reverent
reverential
reverie
reversal
reverse
reversibility
reversible
reversion
reversionary
revert
reverted
revertible
revetment
revictual
review
reviewed
reviewer
revile
reviled
revilement
revilingly
revise
revised
reviser

revision
revisit
revitalization
revitalize
revival
revive
revived
revivification
revivify
revocable
revocation
revoke
revolt
revolted
revoltingly
revolution
revolutionary
revolutionist
revolutionize
revolve
revolved
revolver
revulsion
revulsive
reward
rewarded
rewardingly
rewrite
rewritten
rhapsodic
rhapsodist

rhapsodize
rhapsody
rhenium
rheostat
rhesus
rhetoric
rhetorical
rhetorician
rheum
rheumatic
rheumatism
rheumatoid
rhinal
rhinestone
rhinitis
rhinoceros
rhinology
rhodium
rhomboid
rhombus
rhubarb
rhyme
rhythm
rhythmic
rhythmical
Rialto
rib
ribald
ribaldry
ribbon
rice

rich
richer
riches
richest
richly
richness
rickets
ricochet
riddance
ridden
riddle
ride
rider
riderless
ridge
ridicule
ridiculed
ridiculous
ridiculously
riffraff
riffle
riffled
rifled
rifleman
rigger
right
righteous
righteously
righteousness
rightful
rightfully

rightly
rightness
rigid
rigidity
rigidly
rigidness
rigor
rigorous
rile
riled
rill
rim
rime
rind
ring
ringbolt
ringbone
ringed
ringer
ringingly
ringleader
ringlet
ringlets
ringmaster
ringside
rink
rinse
riot
riotous
riotously
riotousness

rip
riparian
ripe
ripely
ripen
ripened
riper
ripest
ripple
ripply
riprap
rise
risen
riser
risibility
risk
risky
rite
ritual
ritualistic
ritually
rival
rivalry
river
riverside
rivet
rivulet
roach
road
roadbed
roadhouse

roadstead
roadster
roadway
roam
roamed
roamer
roamings
roar
roared
roarings
roast
roaster
rob
robber
robbery
robin
robust
robustly
robustness
rock
rocker
rocket
rockweed
rocky
rococo
rod
rodent
rodeo
rodman
roe
rogue

roguery
roguish
roguishly
roil
roister
roisterer
roll
rolled
roller
romaine
Roman
romance
Romanesque
romantic
romantically
romanticism
romp
rompers
rondeau
roof
roofer
roofless
rooftree
rook
rookery
room
roomed
roomer
roomful
roominess
roommate

roomy
roost
rooster
root
rooted
rooter
rootlet
rootlets
rope
roquet
rosaceous
rosary
rose
roseate
rosette
rosewood
rosily
rosin
rosiness
roster
rostrum
rosy
rot
Rotarian
rotary
rotate
rotated
rotation
rotative
rotator
rotatory

rote
rotenone
rotogravure
rotor
rotten
rottenness
rotund
rotunda
rotundity
rouge
rough
roughage
roughcast
roughdry
roughen
roughened
rougher
roughest
roughhew
roughly
roughneck
roughness
roughrider
roulade
roulette
round
rounder
roundest
roundhouse
roundly
roundness

roundsman
roundworm
rouse
roused
rousingly
rout
route
routed
routed
routine
rover
rovings
row
row
rowboat
rowdy
rowed
rowel
rowen
rower
rowlock
royal
royalism
royalist
royally
royalty
rub
rubber
rubberize
rubbery
rubbings

rubbish
rubicund
ruble
rubric
ruby
rucksack
rudder
ruddily
ruddiness
ruddy
rude
rudely
rudeness
ruder
rudest
rudiment
rudimental
rudimentary
rueful
ruff
ruffian
ruffle
ruffled
Rugby
rugged
ruin
ruination
ruined
ruinous
rule
ruled

ruler
rulings
rum
rumble
ruminant
ruminate
rumination
ruminative
rummage
rumor
rumored
rump
rumple
rumpus
run
runabout
rune

rung
runic
runner
runt
runway
rupee
rupture
ruptured
rural
ruralize
rurally
ruse
rush
rushingly
rusk
russet
Russian

rust
rustic
rusticate
rustication
rusticity
rustily
rustiness
rustle
rustled
rustler
rustlingly
rusty
rut
rutabaga
ruthenium
ruthless
rye

S

Sabbatarian
Sabbath
sabbatical
saber
sable
sabotage
saccharin
sachem
sachet
sack
sackcloth
sackful
sacral
sacrament
sacramental
sacred
sacredly
sacredness
sacrifice
sacrificed
sacrificial
sacrilege
sacrilegious
sacristan
sacristy
sacrosanct
sacrum

sad
sadden
sadder
saddest
saddle
saddlebag
saddler
saddlery
sadiron
sadly
sadness
safe
safeguard
safekeeping
safely
safeness
safer
safest
safety
saffron
sag
saga
sagacious
sagaciously
sagacity
sagamore
sage

sagittal
sago
sahib
said
sail
sailboat
sailfish
sailings
sailor
saint
sainted
sainthood
saintliness
saintly
sake
salaam
salability
salable
salacious
salaciously
salaciousness
salad
salamander
salary
sale
saleratus
salesman

salience
salient
saliferous
saline
saliva
salivate
salivation
sallow
sally
salmon
saloon
salsify
salt
saltcellar
salted
saltpeter
salty
salubrious
salubrity
salutary
salutation
salutatorian
salutatory
salute
saluted
salvage
salvaged
salvation
salve
salve
salver

salvo
Samaritan
samarium
same
sameness
samite
Samoan
samovar
sampan
sample
sampled
sampler
samplings
samurai
sanatorium
sanatory
sanctification
sanctify
sanctimonious
sanctimoniously
sanctimoniousness
sanction
sanctitude
sanctity
sanctuary
sanctum
sand
sandal
sandbag
sandblast
sandiness

sandman
sandpaper
sandpiper
sandstone
sandwich
sandy
sane
sanely
sanguinary
sanguine
sanitarium
sanitary
sanitation
sanity
Sanskrit
sap
sapience
sapient
sapling
saponification
saponify
sapper
sapphire
sapwood
saraband
Saracen
sarcasm
sarcastic
sarcastically
sarcoma
sarcophagi

sarcophagus
sardine
Sardinian
sardonic
sardonically
sardonyx
sarong
sarsaparilla
sartorial
sash
sassafras
sat
Satan
satanic
satchel
sateen
satellite
satiate
satiation
satiety
satin
satinette
satire
satiric
satirical
satirically
satirist
satirize
satirized
satisfaction
satisfactorily

satisfactory
satisfied
satisfy
satisfyingly
satrap
saturate
saturated
saturation
Saturday
Saturn
saturnine
satyr
sauce
saucepan
saucer
saucily
saucy
saunter
sauntered
saunterer
saurian
sausage
sauterne
savable
savage
savagely
savagery
savanna
savant
save
saved

savings
savior
savor
savorless
savory
saw
sawdust
sawed
sawfly
sawhorse
sawmill
sawn
Saxon
say
sayings
says
scab
scabbard
scabby
scabies
scabrous
scaffold
scald
scalded
scale
scaled
scalene
scallion
scallop
scalp
scalpel

scaly
scamp
scamper
scan
scandal
scandalization
scandalize
scandalized
scandalous
scandalously
Scandinavian
scandium
scansion
scansorial
scant
scantily
scantiness
scantling
scanty
scapegoat
scaphoid
scapula
scapular
scar
scarab
scarce
scarcely
scarcity
scare
scared
scarf

scarification
scarify
scarlatina
scarlet
scathing
scathingly
scatter
scattered
scatteringly
scavenger
scenario
scene
scenery
scenic
scenical
scent
scented
scepter
sceptered
schedule
scheduled
schematic
schematize
scheme
schemed
schemer
scherzo
schism
schismatic
schismatical
schist

schizoid
schizophrenia
scholar
scholarly
scholarship
scholastic
scholasticism
scholium
school
schoolbook
schoolboy
schoolhouse
schoolmaster
schoolmate
schoolroom
schoolwork
schoolyard
schooner
schottische
sciatica
science
scientific
scientifically
scientist
scimitar
scintillant
scintillate
scintillated
scintillation
scion
scissors

scleritis
sclerosis
sclerotic
sclerotitis
sclerotomy
scoff
scoffed
scoffer
scoffingly
scold
scolded
scoldings
scone
scoop
scoot
scooter
scope
scopolamine
scorch
scorcher
scorchingly
score
scored
scorn
scorned
scornful
scornfully
scorpion
Scot
Scotch
scoundrel

scoundrelly
scour
scoured
scourge
scourged
scourings
scout
scouted
scow
scowl
scowled
scowlingly
scramble
scrap
scrapbook
scraper
scrapings
scrapple
scrappy
scratch
scratchiness
scratchy
scrawl
scrawled
scrawniness
scrawny
scream
screamed
screech
screechy
screed

screen
screened
screenings
screw
screwed
scribble
scribbler
scribe
scrimmage
scrimp
scrip
script
scriptural
scripture
scrivener
scrod
scrofula
scrofulous
scroll
scrollwork
scrub
scrubbed
scrubbings
scrubby
scrummage
scruple
scrupulosity
scrupulous
scrupulously
scrupulousness
scrutinize

scrutinized
scrutinizingly
scrutiny
scud
scudded
scuff
scuffle
scull
sculled
scullery
scullion
sculpin
sculptor
sculptural
sculpture
sculpturesque
scum
scupper
scurrility
scurrilous
scurrilously
scurry
scurvy
scuttle
scuttled
scythe
sea
seaboard
seacoast
seafarer
seafowl

seal
sealed
sealer
sealskin
seam
seaman
seamanship
seamless
seamstress
seamy
seaplane
seaport
sear
search
searcher
searchingly
searchlight
seared
seascape
seashore
seasick
seasickness
seaside
season
seasonable
seasonal
seasonally
seasoned
seasonings
seat
seated

seaward
sebaceous
secant
secede
secession
secessionist
seclude
secluded
seclusion
second
secondarily
secondary
seconded
seconder
secondhand
secondly
secrecy
secret
secretarial
secretariat
secretary
secrete
secreted
secretion
secretive
secretively
secretly
secretory
sect
sectarian
sectarianism

sectary
section
sectional
sectionalism
sectionalize
sectionalized
sectionally
sector
secular
secularism
secularize
secularized
secure
secured
securely
security
sedan
sedate
sedately
sedateness
sedative
sedentary
sedge
sediment
sedimentary
sedimentation
sedition
seditious
seditiously
seditiousness
seduce
seducer
seducible
seduction
seductive
seductively
seductiveness
sedulous
sedulously
sedum
see
seed
seediness
seedling
seedy
seek
seeker
seem
seemed
seemingly
seemliness
seemly
seep
seepage
seersucker
seesaw
seethe
seethed
segment
segmental
segmentary
segmentation
segregate
segregated
segregation
seguidilla
seine
seismic
seismograph
seismology
seizable
seize
seizure
seldom
select
selected
selection
selective
selectivity
selectmen
selector
selenate
selenide
selenite
selenium
self
self-assertion
self-assured
self-colored
self-command
self-complacency
self-complacent
self-conceit

self-confidence
self-conscious
self-consciousness
self-contained
self-contradiction
self-contradictory
self-control
self-deceit
self-defense
self-denial
self-destruction
self-determination
self-determined
self-educated
self-esteem
self-evident
self-examination
self-executing
self-explaining
self-explanatory
self-government
self-help
self-importance
self-induced
self-indulgence
self-indulgent
self-interest
selfish
selfishly
selfishness
self-love

self-made
self-opinionated
self-perception
self-possessed
self-possession
self-registering
self-reliance
self-reliant
self-renunciation
self-reproach
self-reproachful
self-respect
self-restraint
self-righteous
self-righteousness
self-sacrifice
selfsame
self-satisfied
self-seeker
self-service
self-starter
self-styled
self-sufficiency
self-sufficient
self-surrender
self-sustaining
self-winding
sell
sellout
Seltzer
selvage

semantic
semaphore
semblance
semester
semiannual
semicircle
semicircular
semicivilized
semicolon
semidetached
semifinal
semimonthly
seminar
seminary
Seminole
semiofficial
semiopaque
semiprecious
Semite
Semitic
Semitism
semitone
semitranslucent
semitransparent
semiweekly
semolina
sempiternal
senate
senator
senatorial
senatorially

senatorship
send
sender
Seneca
senescence
senescent
senile
senility
senior
seniority
senna
sennit
sensate
sensation
sensational
sensationalism
sensationally
sense
senseless
senselessly
senselessness
sensibility
sensible
sensitive
sensitively
sensitiveness
sensitivity
sensitization
sensitize
sensitizer
sensory

sensual
sensualism
sensuality
sensually
sensuous
sensuously
sensuousness
sentence
sentenced
sententious
sententiously
sententiousness
sentience
sentiency
sentient
sentiently
sentiment
sentimental
sentimentalism
sentimentalist
sentimentalists
sentimentality
sentimentally
sentinel
sentry
separability
separable
separate
separated
separately
separation

separatist
separatists
separative
separator
sepia
sepoy
sepsis
September
septennial
septet
septic
septicemia
septum
sepulcher
sepulchral
sepulture
sequel
sequela
sequelae
sequence
sequential
sequentially
sequester
sequestered
sequestrate
sequestrated
sequestration
sequin
sequoia
seraglio
seraph

seraphic
seraphical
seraphim
Serbian
serenade
serenaded
serenata
serene
serenely
sereneness
serenity
serf
serfdom
serge
sergeant
serial
serially
sericulture
series
serif
serious
seriously
seriousness
sermon
sermonize
sermonized
serous
serpent
serpentine
serpiginous
serum

servant
serve
served
server
service
serviceability
serviceable
serviceably
servile
servility
servings
servitor
servitude
sesame
session
set
setback
setoff
settee
setter
settings
settle
settled
settlement
settler
sever
severable
several
severally
severalty
severance

severe
severely
severity
sew
sewage
sewed
sewer
sewerage
sewn
sextant
sextet
sexton
shabbiness
shabby
shack
shackle
shackled
shade
shaded
shadier
shadiest
shadily
shadiness
shadings
shadow
shadowy
shady
shaft
shag
shaggy
shake

shaken
shaker
Shakespearean
shakily
shakiness
shako
shaky
shale
shall
shallop
shallot
shallow
shallowly
shallowness
sham
shamble
shame
shamed
shamefaced
shameful
shamefully
shamefulness
shameless
shamelessly
shamelessness
shampoo
shamrock
shanghai
shank
shan't
shanty

shape
shapeless
shapelessly
shapelessness
shapeliness
shapely
shard
share
shared
sharer
shareholder
shark
sharp
sharpen
sharpened
sharpener
sharper
sharpest
sharply
sharpness
sharpshooter
shatter
shattered
shave
shaver
shavings
shawl
Shawnee
she
sheaf
shear

sheared
shearings
shears
sheathe
sheathed
sheave
shed
sheen
sheep
sheepish
sheepishly
sheepishness
sheepskin
sheer
sheerer
sheerest
sheet
sheetings
shelf
shell
shellac
shellfish
shellproof
shelter
sheltered
shelterless
shelve
shelved
shepherd
Sheraton
sherbet

sheriff
sherry
shibboleth
shield
shift
shiftily
shiftiness
shiftless
shifty
shim
shimmer
shimmered
shimmery
shin
shine
shiner
shingle
shingled
Shinto
shiny
ship
shipboard
shipbuilder
shipload
shipmaster
shipmate
shipment
shipowner
shipper
shipshape
shipworm

shipwreck
shipwright
shipyard
shire
shirk
shirker
shirr
shirred
shirt
shirtings
shiver
shivered
shoal
shock
shockingly
shoddy
shoe
shoes
shook
shoot
shootings
shop
shopkeeper
shoplifter
shopman
shopper
shopworn
shore
shored
shorn
short

shortage
shortcake
shortchange
shortcomings
shorten
shorter
shortest
shorthand
shortly
shortness
shortsighted
shortstop
shot
should
shoulder
shouldered
shout
shouted
shove
shovel
shoveled
shovelhead
show
showboat
showed
shower
showered
showily
showiness
showings
showman

shown
showroom
showy
shrank
shrapnel
shred
shrew
shrewd
shrewdly
shrewdness
shriek
shrift
shrike
shrill
shrillness
shrilly
shrimp
shrine
shrink
shrinkage
shrinkingly
shrive
shrivel
shriveled
shroud
shrub
shrubbery
shrug
shrunk
shrunken
shuck

shudder
shuddered
shudderingly
shuffle
shuffled
shun
shunned
shunt
shut
shutdown
shutoff
shutout
shutter
shuttered
shuttle
shuttled
shy
shyly
shyness
shyster
sialagogue
Siamese
sibilance
sibilant
sibyl
sibylline
Sicilian
sick
sickbed
sicken
sickened

sickeningly
sicker
sickest
sickle
sickliness
sickly
sickness
side
sideboard
sidelong
sidepiece
sides
sidereal
siderite
sidesaddle
sidetrack
sidewalk
sidings
sidle
sidled
siege
Sienna
sierra
siesta
sieve
sift
sifted
sigh
sight
sighted
sightless

sightliness
sightly
sigmoid
signal
signaled
signalize
signalized
signally
signatory
signature
signboard
signed
signer
signet
significance
significant
significantly
signification
signify
signpost
silage
silence
silenced
silencer
silent
silently
silentness
silex
silhouette
silica
silicate

silicon
silicosis
silk
silken
silkiness
silkweed
silkworm
silky
sill
sillabub
silliness
silly
silo
silt
silvan
silver
silversmith
silverware
silvery
simian
similar
similarity
similarly
simile
similitude
simmer
simmered
simony
simoom
simoon
simper

simpered
simple
simpler
simplest
simpleton
simplicity
simplification
simplify
simply
simulacrum
simulate
simulation
simultaneous
simultaneously
sin
since
sincere
sincerely
sincerity
sine
sinecure
sinew
sinewy
sinful
sing
singable
singe
singer
single
singled
singleness

singly
singular
singularity
singularly
sinister
sinistral
sink
sinker
sinless
sinlessly
sinned
sinner
sinuosity
sinuous
sinus
sinusitis
Sioux
sip
siphon
siphoned
sir
sire
siren
sirloin
sirocco
sirup
sister
sisterhood
sister-in-law
sisterly
sit

site
sitter
sittings
situated
situation
sixth
sizable
size
sized
sizes
sizzle
skate
skater
skein
skeletal
skeleton
skeletonize
skeptic
skeptical
skepticism
sketch
sketchily
sketchy
skew
skewer
ski
skid
skiff
skill
skilled
skillful

skillfully
skim
skimmed
skimmer
skimpy
skinflint
skinny
skip
skipper
skirmish
skirmisher
skirt
skitter
skittish
skittishly
skittishness
skittles
skiver
skulk
skull
skunk
sky
skylark
skylight
skyrocket
skyscraper
skyward
slab
slack
slacken
slackened

slackness
slag
slain
slake
slam
slammed
slander
slandered
slanderer
slanderous
slang
slangy
slant
slanted
slantingly
slap
slapdash
slash
slat
slattern
slatternly
slaughter
slaughtered
slaughterer
slaughterhouse
slave
slavery
slavish
slaw
slay
slayer

slayings
sleaziness
sleazy
sled
sledge
sleek
sleekly
sleekness
sleep
sleeper
sleepily
sleepiness
sleepless
sleeplessness
sleepy
sleet
sleeve
sleigh
sleight
slender
slenderer
slenderest
slenderness
slept
sleuth
slew
slice
sliced
slicer
slick
slicker

slid
slide
slier
sliest
slight
slighter
slightest
slightingly
slightly
slightness
slim
slime
slimily
sliminess
slimmer
slimmest
slimness
slimy
sling
slink
slinkiest
slip
slipknot
slippage
slipper
slipperiness
slippery
slipshod
slit
slither
sliver

slob
slobber
sloe
slog
slogan
sloop
slop
sloppy
slosh
slot
sloth
slothful
slothfully
slothfulness
slouch
slouchily
slouchiness
slouchy
slough
slough
slovenliness
slovenly
slow
slower
slowest
slowly
slowness
sloyd
sludge
slug
sluggard
slugger
sluggish
sluggishly
sluggishness
sluice
sluiceway
slum
slumber
slumbered
slumberer
slumberous
slump
slung
slur
slurred
slush
slushy
sly
slyly
smack
small
smaller
smallest
smallness
smallpox
smart
smarten
smarter
smartest
smartly
smartness
smash
smashup
smatter
smear
smeared
smell
smelled
smelt
smelter
smilax
smile
smiled
smilingly
smirch
smirk
smite
smith
smithy
smitten
smock
smoke
smokeless
smoker
smokestack
smokiest
smoky
smolder
smoldered
smooth
smoothed
smoother

smoothest
smoothly
smoothness
smote
smother
smothered
smudge
smug
smuggle
smuggled
smuggler
smugly
smugness
smut
smuttiest
smutty
snack
snaffle
snag
snail
snake
snaky
snap
snapdragon
snapper
snappish
snappy
snapshot
snare
snared
snarl

snarled
snatch
snath
sneak
sneaker
sneakiest
sneaky
sneer
sneered
sneeringly
sneeze
sneezed
sneezeweed
snicker
snickered
sniff
sniffle
sniffled
snip
snipe
snob
snobbery
snobbish
snobbishly
snobbishness
snood
snoop
snoot
snooze
snore
snored

snort
snout
snow
snowball
snowbound
snowdrift
snowdrop
snowfall
snowflake
snowiness
snowplow
snowshed
snowshoe
snowslide
snowslip
snowstorm
snowy
snub
snuff
snuffer
snuffle
snug
snuggery
snuggle
snuggled
snugly
snugness
so
soak
soap
soapiness

soapstone
soapy
soar
soared
sob
sober
soberly
sobriety
sobriquet
soccer
sociability
sociable
sociably
social
socialism
socialist
socialistic
socialization
socialize
socialized
socially
socialness
society
sociological
sociology
sock
socket
Socratic
sod
soda
sodality

sodden
sodium
sofa
soft
soften
softer
softest
softly
softness
soggy
soil
soiled
sojourn
sojourned
solace
solar
solarium
solder
soldier
soldierly
soldiery
sole
solecism
solely
solemn
solemnity
solemnization
solemnize
solemnly
solenoid
solicit

solicitation
solicitor
solicitous
solicitude
solid
solidarity
solidification
solidify
solidity
solidly
solidness
soliloquize
soliloquy
solitaire
solitary
solitude
solo
soloist
solstice
solubility
soluble
solution
solvable
solve
solvency
solvent
somber
sombrero
some
somebody
somehow

someone
somersault
something
sometime
somewhat
somewhere
somnambulism
somnambulist
somnolent
son
sonata
song
songster
sonic
son-in-law
sonnet
sonority
sonorous
soon
sooner
soonest
soot
soothe
soothed
soothingly
soothsayer
sooty
sop
sophism
sophist
sophisticate
sophistication
sophistry
sophomore
soporific
soprano
sorcerer
sorcery
sordid
sordidness
sore
sorely
sorghum
sorority
sorosis
sorrow
sorrowful
sorrowfully
sorry
sort
sorted
sorter
sortie
soubrette
sought
soul
soulful
soulless
soullessly
soullessness
sound
sounded
soundless
soundly
soundness
soup
sour
source
soured
souse
south
southeast
southeasterly
southeastern
southerly
southern
southerner
southernmost
southward
southwest
southwesterly
souvenir
sovereign
sovereignty
Soviet
sow
sow
soy
soya
spa
space
spacious
spaciously

spaciousness
spade
spadefish
spaghetti
span
spandrel
spangle
spangled
spaniel
Spanish
spank
spanked
spankings
spanner
spare
spared
sparerib
sparingly
spark
sparkle
sparkled
sparklingly
sparrow
sparse
sparsely
sparsity
Spartan
spasm
spasmodic
spasmodically
spastic

spatter
spattered
spatula
spatulate
spawn
spawned
speak
speaker
spear
speared
spearfish
spearhead
special
specialist
specialization
specialize
specialized
specially
specialty
specie
species
specific
specifically
specification
specify
specimen
specious
speciously
speciousness
speck
speckle

speckled
spectacle
spectacular
spectacularly
spectator
specter
spectral
spectroscope
spectrum
speculate
speculated
speculates
speculation
speculative
speculator
speculatory
speculum
speech
speechless
speechlessly
speechlessness
speed
speedboat
speedily
speedometer
speedway
speedy
spell
spellbound
spelled
speller

spellings
spelt
spend
spendthrift
spent
spermaceti
spew
sphagnum
sphere
spherical
spheroid
sphinx
spice
spiced
spiciness
spicy
spider
spidery
spigot
spike
spill
spilled
spillway
spin
spinach
spinal
spindle
spine
spineless
spinet
spinnaker

spinner
spinneret
spinster
spinsterhood
spiny
spiral
spiraled
spirally
spire
spired
spirit
spirited
spiritual
spiritualism
spiritualist
spirituality
spiritualize
spiritually
spirituous
spirochete
spit
spite
spiteful
spittoon
splash
spleen
splendid
splendidly
splendor
splendorous
splenetic

splice
splicer
splint
splinter
split
splurge
splutter
spoil
spoilage
spoiled
spoke
spoken
spokeshave
spokesman
spoliation
spoliative
spoliator
spondee
sponge
sponger
spongy
sponsor
sponsorship
spontaneity
spontaneous
spook
spool
spoon
spoonful
spoor
sporadic

spore
sport
sportive
sportsman
sportsmanship
sporty
spot
spotless
spotlessly
spotlessness
spotlight
spotted
spotter
spotty
spouse
spout
sprain
sprained
sprawl
sprawled
spray
sprayer
spread
spreader
spree
sprig
sprightliness
sprightly
spring
springboard
springtime
springy
sprinkle
sprinkled
sprinkler
sprint
sprinter
sprite
spritsail
sprocket
sprout
spruce
sprung
spry
spud
spume
spun
spunk
spunky
spur
spurred
spurious
spuriously
spurn
spurned
spurt
spurted
sputter
sputtered
sputum
spy
squab
squad
squadron
squalid
squalidity
squalidly
squall
squalor
squander
square
squared
squarehead
squarely
squareness
squash
squat
squatter
squaw
squawfish
squeak
squeal
squealed
squeamish
squeegee
squeeze
squeezed
squelch
squib
squid
squint
squire
squirm

squirmed
squirmings
squirrel
squirt
stab
stability
stabilization
stabilize
stabilized
stabilizer
stable
staccato
stack
stadia
stadium
staff
stag
stage
stagecoach
stagecraft
stagger
staggered
stagnant
stagnate
stagnation
staid
stain
stained
stainless
stair
staircase
stairway
stake
stalactite
stalagmite
stale
stalemate
stalk
stall
stalled
stallion
stamen
stamina
stammer
stammered
stammerer
stamp
stampede
stampeded
stampings
stanch
stanchion
stand
standard
standardization
standardize
standpipe
standpoint
standstill
stank
stannate
stannic
stannous
stanza
staple
stapler
star
starboard
starch
starchy
stare
stared
starfish
stark
starless
starlight
starling
starred
starry
start
started
starter
startle
startled
starvation
starve
state
stated
statehood
statehouse
stateliness
stately
statement

stateroom
statesman
static
station
stationary
stationer
stationery
statistical
statistically
statistician
statistics
statuary
statue
statuesque
statuette
stature
status
statute
statutory
stave
stay
stayed
stead
steadfast
steadfastly
steadfastness
steadier
steadiest
steadily
steadiness
steady

steak
steal
stealth
stealthily
steam
steamboat
steamed
steamer
steampipe
steamship
steamy
steatite
steel
steelwork
steep
steeper
steepest
steeple
steeplechase
steeply
steepness
steer
steerage
steered
steersman
stein
stellar
stem
stemmed
stench
stencil

stenciled
stenographer
stenographic
stenography
stenosis
stentorian
step
stepchild
stepdaughter
stepladder
stepmother
steppe
stepped
stepson
stereopticon
stereoscope
stereotype
sterile
sterility
sterilization
sterilize
sterilized
sterilizer
sterling
stern
sterner
sternest
sternly
sternness
sternpost
sternum

sternutation stertorous stet stethoscope stevedore stew steward stick sticker stickful stickier stickiest stickiness stickler stickpin stickweed sticky stiff stiffen stiffened stiffness stifle stifled stiflingly stigma stigmas stigmata stigmatic stigmatism stigmatize stile

stiletto still stillborn stillness stilly stilt stilted stimulant stimulate stimulated stimulates stimulation stimuli stimulus sting stinger stingier stingiest stingily stinginess stingy stink stinker stinkpot stinkweed stint stinted stipend stipendiary stipple stippled

stipulate stipulated stipulates stipulation stir stirred stirringly stirrings stirrup stitch stoat stock stockade stockbroker stockholder stockily stockiness stockinet stockings stockman stocky stockyard stogy stoic stoical stoicism stoke stokehold stoker stole stolen

stolid
stolidity
stolidly
stomach
stone
stoned
stoneware
stonework
stonily
stoniness
stony
stood
stool
stoop
stop
stopgap
stoppage
stopped
stopper
stopple
storage
store
stored
storehouse
storeroom
stork
storm
stormed
stormy
story
stout
stouter
stoutest
stouthearted
stoutly
stoutness
stove
stow
stowage
stowaway
strabismus
straddle
straddled
straggle
straggled
straggler
straight
straightedge
straighten
straightened
straightforward
straightforwardness
straightway
strain
strained
strainer
strait
straiten
straitened
strake
strand
stranded
strange
strangely
strangeness
stranger
strangest
strangle
strangled
strangler
strangles
strangulate
strangulated
strangulation
strap
strata
stratagem
strategic
strategical
strategist
strategy
stratification
stratify
stratum
stratus
straw
strawberry
stray
streak
streaky
stream
streamed
streamer

streamlet
streamlets
streamline
street
strength
strengthen
strengthened
strenuous
strenuously
strenuousness
stress
stretch
stretcher
strew
strewed
strewn
striate
striated
striation
stricken
strict
strictly
strictness
stricture
stride
strident
stridently
stridulous
strife
strike
striker

strikingly
string
stringed
stringency
stringent
stringently
stringer
stringpiece
stringy
strip
stripe
stripling
strive
striven
strode
stroke
stroll
strolled
stroller
strong
stronger
strongest
stronghold
strongly
strontium
strop
strophe
strove
struck
structural
structurally

structure
struggle
struggled
struggler
strum
strummed
strumpet
strung
strut
strutted
strutter
strychnine
stub
stubble
stubborn
stubby
stucco
stuck
stud
student
studied
studio
studious
study
stuff
stuffier
stuffiest
stuffiness
stuffy
stultification
stultify

stumble
stump
stun
stunned
stunner
stunningly
stunt
stunted
stupefacient
stupefaction
stupefy
stupendous
stupid
stupidity
stupidly
stupor
sturdily
sturdiness
sturdy
sturgeon
stutter
stuttered
stutterer
sty
style
stylish
stylishness
stylist
stylistic
stylographic
stylus

stymie
styptic
Styx
suasion
suave
suavely
suavity
subacute
subaltern
subaqueous
subarctic
subcaliber
subcellar
subcommittee
subconscious
subconsciously
subconsciousness
subcontract
subcontractor
subcutaneous
subdeacon
subdivide
subdivision
subdue
subeditor
subfamily
subgroup
subhead
subject
subjection
subjective

subjectivity
subjoin
subjoined
subjugate
subjugation
subjunctive
sublease
sublet
sublimate
sublimated
sublimation
sublime
sublimest
subliminal
sublimity
subluxation
submarine
submerge
submersible
submersion
submission
submissive
submit
submitted
subnormal
suboceanic
subordinate
subordination
suborn
subornation
suborner

subpoena
subscribe
subscribed
subscriber
subscription
subsequent
subserve
subservience
subservient
subside
subsidence
subsidiary
subsidize
subsidy
subsist
subsistence
subsists
subsoil
substance
substantial
substantially
substantiate
substantiation
substantive
substitute
substituted
substitution
substratum
substructure
subterfuge
subterranean
subterraneous
subtitle
subtle
subtler
subtlest
subtlety
subtly
subtract
subtracted
subtraction
subtrahend
subtreasury
subtropical
suburb
suburban
suburbanite
subvention
subversion
subversive
subvert
subway
succeed
success
successful
successfully
succession
successive
successor
succinct
succinctly
succor
succotash
succulence
succulent
succumb
such
suck
sucker
suckle
suckled
suction
sudden
suddenly
suddenness
sudoriferous
sudorific
sue
sued
suède
suet
suffer
sufferable
sufferance
suffered
sufferer
sufferings
suffice
sufficiency
sufficient
suffix
suffocate
suffocation

suffragan
suffrage
suffumigate
suffuse
suffusion
sugar
sugared
sugarplum
sugary
suggest
suggestibility
suggestible
suggestion
suggestive
suggestiveness
suicidal
suicide
suicides
suit
suitability
suitable
suite
suitor
sulk
sulkily
sulkiness
sulky
sullen
sullenly
sullenness
sully

sulphate
sulphide
sulphite
sulphur
sulphuric
sulphurous
sultan
sultanate
sultry
sum
sumac
summarily
summariness
summarization
summarize
summary
summation
summed
summer
summerhouse
summery
summit
summon
summoned
sump
sumpter
sumptuary
sumptuous
sumptuously
sumptuousness
sunbeam

sunbonnet
sunburn
sunburst
Sunday
sunder
sundial
sundry
sunfish
sunflower
sunglass
sunk
sunken
sunless
sunlight
sunlit
sunned
sunniness
sunny
sunrise
sunset
sunshade
sunshine
sunspot
sunstroke
sup
superable
superabundant
superannuate
superannuation
superb
supercalender

supercalendered
supercargo
supercharger
supercilious
superciliously
superciliousness
superdreadnought
supereminent
supererogation
superficial
superficiality
superficially
superfluity
superfluous
superfluously
superfluousness
superheat
superhuman
superhumanly
superimpose
superimposition
superinduce
superintend
superintendence
superintendency
superintendent
superior
superiority
superlative
supernatural
supernaturally

supernumerary
superposition
supersaturate
superscription
supersede
superseded
supersensitive
superstition
superstitious
superstructure
supervene
supervened
supervise
supervised
supervision
supervisor
supervisory
supineness
supper
supplant
supplanted
supple
supplement
supplemental
supplementary
suppliant
supplicant
supplicate
supplicated
supplication
supplicatory

supplier
supply
support
supporter
suppose
supposedly
supposition
supposititious
suppository
suppress
suppression
suppressive
suprarenal
supremacy
supreme
supremely
surbase
surcease
surcharge
surcingle
surd
sure
surely
sureness
surety
surf
surface
surfeit
surge
surgeon
surgery

surgical
surly
surmise
surmised
surmount
surname
surpass
surpassingly
surplice
surplus
surprise
surprised
surprisingly
surrebuttal
surrebutter
surrejoinder
surrender
surreptitious
surrey
surrogate
surround
surrounded
surroundings
surtax
surtout
surveillance
survey
surveyed
surveyor
survival
survive

survivorship
susceptibility
susceptible
suspect
suspend
suspended
suspender
suspense
suspension
suspicion
suspicious
sustain
sustained
sustenance
suture
sutured
svelte
swab
swaddle
swaddled
swag
swage
swagger
swaggered
swain
swallow
swamp
swan
swank
swanky
swarm

swarthy
swastika
sway
swayed
swear
sweat
sweatband
sweater
sweatiness
sweatshop
Swedish
sweep
sweeper
sweepingly
sweepings
sweet
sweetbread
sweetbrier
sweeten
sweetened
sweetheart
sweetish
sweetly
sweetmeat
sweetness
swell
swelled
swellings
swelter
sweltered
swelteringly

swerve
swift
swifter
swiftest
swiftly
swiftness
swill
swim
swimmingly
swindle
swindled
swindler
swine
swineherd
swing
swipe
swirl
swirled
swish
Swiss
switch
switchboard
switchman
swivel
swollen
swoon
swoop
sword
swordfish
swum
swung

sybarite
sycamore
sycophancy
sycophant
sycophantic
syllabi
syllabic
syllabicate
syllabication
syllabification
syllabify
syllable
syllabus
syllabuses
syllogism
syllogistic
sylph
sylvan
symbol
symbolic
symbolical
symbolism
symbolist
symbolize
symmetrical
symmetry
sympathetic
sympathize
sympathizer
sympathy
symphony

symposium
symptom
symptomatic
synagogue
synchronize
synchronous
syncopate
syncopation
syncope
syndic
syndicalism
syndicate
syndrome
synod
synonym
synonymous
synopsis
synoptic
syntax
synthesis
synthesize
synthetic
synthetically
syringe
system
systematic
systematize
systemic
systole
systolic
syzygy

T

tabasco
tabernacle
tabes
table
tableau
tablecloth
tablet
tablets
tableware
tabloid
taboo
tabor
tabular
tabulate
tabulation
tabulator
tachometer
tacit
tacitly
taciturn
taciturnity
tack
tackle
tackled
tact
tactful
tactical
tactician
tactics
tactile
tactless
tactlessly
tadpole
taffeta
taffrail
taffy
tag
tagged
tail
tailboard
tailings
tailless
tailor
tailpiece
tailrace
tailstock
taint
tainted
take
takedown
taken
taker
takings
talc
talcum
tale
talebearer
talent
talented
talisman
talk
talkative
talker
tall
taller
tallest
tallish
tallness
tallow
tally
Talmud
talon
tamarack
tamarind
tambourine
tame
tamed
tamer
tamest
tameness
tamper

tampered
tampon
tan
tanager
tandem
tang
tangent
tangential
tangentiality
tangerine
tangible
tangle
tangled
tango
tank
tankage
tankard
tanker
tanner
tannery
tannic
tantalization
tantalize
tantalized
tantalum
Tantalus
tantamount
tantrum
tap
taper
tapered

tapestry
tapeworm
tapioca
tapir
tappet
tar
tarantella
tarantula
tardier
tardiest
tardy
tare
target
tariff
tarlatan
tarnish
tarnished
tarpaulin
tarpon
tarragon
tarred
tarry
tart
tartan
task
taskmaster
Tasmanian
tassel
tasseled
taste
tasted

tasteful
tastefully
tasteless
tastily
tasty
tatter
tattered
tattle
tattled
tattoo
tattooed
taunt
taunted
tauntingly
taut
tautological
tautology
tavern
tawdry
tawny
tax
taxable
taxation
taxed
taxes
taxi
taxicab
taxidermist
taxidermy
taximeter
taxpayer

teach
teachability
teachable
teacher
teacherage
teachings
teacup
teakettle
team
teamster
teamwork
tear
tear
tearful
tearless
tease
teased
teasingly
teaspoon
teaspoonful
technical
technicality
technician
technique
technological
technology
tedious
tediously
tedium
teeter
teetered

teeth
teetotal
teetotaler
telautograph
telecast
telegram
telegraph
telegrapher
telegraphic
telegraphy
telepathic
telepathy
telephone
telephonic
telescope
telescopic
teletype
teleview
televise
television
tell
teller
tellingly
tellings
telltale
tellurium
temerity
temper
temperament
temperamental
temperamentally

temperance
temperate
temperately
temperature
tempest
tempestuous
template
temple
tempo
temporal
temporarily
temporary
temporize
temporized
temporizer
tempt
temptation
tempted
tempter
temptingly
temptress
tenability
tenable
tenacious
tenacity
tenancy
tenant
tenantable
tenanted
tenantless
tenantry

tend
tended
tendency
tender
tendered
tenderer
tenderest
tenderfoot
tenderloin
tenderly
tenderness
tendon
tendril
tenement
tenet
tennis
tenon
tenor
tense
tensile
tension
tent
tentacle
tentative
tenterhooks
tenuity
tenuous
tenuously
tenure
tepee
tepid

tepidity
tercentenary
teredo
tergiversate
term
termagant
termed
terminable
terminal
terminate
terminated
termination
terminology
terminus
termite
termless
tern
ternary
terrace
terraced
terrain
terrapin
terrestrial
terrible
terribly
terrier
terrific
terrifically
terrify
territorial
territory

terror
terrorism
terrorist
terroristic
terrorization
terrorize
terse
terseness
tertiary
tessellation
test
testament
testamentary
testator
testify
testimonial
testimony
tests
tetanus
tether
tetragon
tetragonal
tetralogy
Teutonic
text
textbook
textile
textual
textually
texture
thalamic

thalamus
thalassic
thallium
than
thank
thankful
thankfully
thankfulness
thankless
thanklessly
thanksgiving
that
thatch
thaw
the
theater
theatrical
theatrically
theatricals
theft
their
theirs
theism
them
theme
themselves
then
thence
thenceforth
thenceforward
theocracy

theodolite
theologian
theological
theologically
theology
theoretic
theoretical
theoretically
theorist
theorize
theorizer
theory
theosophic
theosophical
theosophist
theosophy
therapeutic
therapeutical
therapy
there
thereabout
thereafter
thereat
thereby
therefore
therefrom
therein
thereof
thereon
thereto
theretofore

thereunto
thereupon
therewith
therm
thermal
thermion
thermite
thermometer
thermometric
thermometrical
thermostat
thesaurus
these
theses
thesis
thew
they
thick
thicken
thickened
thickener
thicker
thickest
thicket
thickly
thickness
thief
thievery
thievish
thigh
thill

thimble
thin
thing
things
think
thinkable
thinker
thinly
thinner
thinness
thinnest
third
thirst
thirstily
thirstiness
thirsty
this
thistle
thither
thole
thong
thoracic
thorax
thorium
thorn
thorny
thorough
thoroughbred
thoroughfare
thoroughly
thoroughness

those
thou
though
thought
thoughtful
thoughtless
thoughtlessly
thoughtlessness
thousand
thousandfold
thrall
thrash
thrashed
thread
threadbare
threadworm
threat
threaten
threatened
threateningly
three
threnody
thresh
threshold
threw
thrice
thrift
thriftily
thriftless
thriftlessness
thrifty

thrill
thrillingly
throat
throatily
throatiness
throaty
throb
thrombosis
thrombus
throne
throng
throttle
throttled
through
throughout
throw
thrown
thrum
thrummed
thrush
thrust
thud
thug
thulium
thumb
thump
thunder
thunderbolt
thundered
thunderous
thundershower

Thursday
thus
thwack
thwart
thy
thyme
thymus
thyroid
thyself
tiara
tibia
tick
ticker
ticket
tickle
tickled
tickler
ticklish
tidal
tide
tidewater
tideway
tidily
tidiness
tidings
tidy
tie
tier
tiffin
tiger
tight
tighten
tightened
tightener
tighter
tightest
tightly
tightrope
tightwad
tile
tiled
till
tiller
tilt
tilted
timber
time
timed
timekeeper
timeless
timeliness
timely
timepiece
timer
timetable
timid
timidity
timidly
timorous
timorously
tin
tinct
tincture
tinctured
tinder
tine
tinge
tinged
tingle
tingled
tinker
tinkle
tinkled
tinned
tinnitus
tinny
tinsel
tinsmith
tint
tinted
tintinnabulation
tinware
tiny
tip
tippet
tipple
tippler
tipsy
tiptoe
tiptop
tirade
tire
tired

tireless
tirelessly
tiresome
tiresomely
tiresomeness
tissue
Titan
titanic
titaniferous
titanium
tithe
titillate
titillated
titillation
titivate
titivated
titivation
title
titled
titmouse
titrate
titration
titter
tittered
titular
titulary
to
toad
toadfish
toadstool
toady

toast
toasted
tobacco
toboggan
toccata
tocsin
today
toddle
toddled
toddy
toe
toenail
toffee
toga
together
toggle
toil
toiled
toiler
toilet
toilets
token
told
tolerable
tolerance
tolerant
tolerate
tolerated
toleration
toll
tomahawk

tomato
tomb
tomboy
tombstone
tomorrow
ton
tonal
tonality
tone
toneless
tongs
tongue
tonic
tonight
tonnage
tonneau
tonsil
tonsillitis
tonsorial
tonsure
tontine
too
took
tool
tooth
toothache
toothbrush
toothed
toothless
toothpick
toothsome

top
topaz
topcoat
topiary
topic
topical
topknot
topmast
topmost
topographer
topographic
topographical
topography
topple
toppled
topsail
toque
torch
torchwood
tore
toreador
torment
tormented
tormentingly
tormentor
tornado
torpedo
torpid
torpidity
torpidly
torpor

torque
torrent
torrential
torrentially
torrid
torridity
torsion
torso
tort
tortoise
tortuously
tortuousness
torture
tortured
torturer
Tory
toss
tossup
total
totaled
totalitarian
totality
totalization
totally
totem
totter
tottered
totteringly
tottery
toucan
touch

touchable
touchdown
touchily
touchiness
touchingly
touchstone
touchy
tough
toughen
toughened
tougher
toughest
tour
toured
tourist
tourists
tourmaline
tournament
tourniquet
tousle
tousled
tow
towage
toward
towards
towboat
towel
tower
towered
toweringly
towline

town
township
toxic
toxicity
toxicology
toxicosis
toy
trace
traceable
tracer
tracery
trachea
tracheal
trachoma
tracings
track
trackage
trackless
trackman
tract
tractability
tractable
traction
tractive
tractor
trade
traded
trader
tradesman
tradition
traditional
traditionally
traffic
trafficked
tragedian
tragedy
tragic
tragical
tragus
trail
trailed
trailer
train
trained
trainer
trainman
trait
traitor
traitorous
traitorously
trajectory
tram
trammel
trammeled
tramp
trample
trampled
tramway
trance
tranquil
tranquillity
tranquilly
transact
transacted
transaction
transatlantic
transcend
transcendence
transcendency
transcendent
transcendental
transcribe
transcribed
transcript
transcription
transept
transfer
transferable
transference
transferred
transfiguration
transfigure
transfigured
transfix
transform
transformation
transformed
transformer
transfusion
transgress
transgression
transgressor
transient

transit
transition
transitional
transitionally
transitive
transitory
translatable
translate
translation
translator
transliterate
translucence
translucent
transmigration
transmissible
transmission
transmit
transmittal
transmitter
transmogrify
transmutable
transmutation
transmute
transmuted
transom
transparency
transparent
transpiration
transpire
transpired
transplant

transplantation
transport
transportation
transported
transposal
transpose
transposed
transposition
transship
transshipment
transubstantiation
transverse
trap
trapdoor
trapeze
trapezoid
trapper
trappings
Trappist
trash
trashy
trauma
traumata
traumatic
travail
travel
traveled
traveler
travelogue
traverse
travesty

trawl
trawler
tray
treacherous
treacherously
treacherousness
treachery
treacle
tread
treadle
treadmill
treason
treasonable
treasure
treasured
treasurer
treasury
treat
treated
treatise
treatment
treaty
treble
tree
trek
trellis
tremble
tremblingly
tremblings
tremendous
tremendously

tremolo
tremor
tremulous
tremulously
tremulousness
trench
trenchancy
trenchant
trenchantly
trencher
trend
trepan
trephine
trepidation
trespass
trespasser
trestle
trestlework
triad
trial
triangle
triangular
triangulate
triangulation
tribal
tribasic
tribe
tribesman
tribulation
tribunal
tribune

tributary
tribute
triceps
trichinosis
trick
trickery
trickily
trickiness
trickle
trickled
trickster
tricky
tricot
tricycle
trident
tried
triennial
trifle
trifled
trifler
trigger
trigonometry
trill
trilled
trillion
trillium
trilogy
trim
trimmed
trimmer
trimness

trinity
trinket
trinomial
trio
trip
tripe
tripthong
triple
triplet
triplets
triplex
triplicate
triplication
triply
tripod
trippingly
trireme
trisect
triturate
trituration
triumph
triumphal
triumphant
triumvir
triumvirate
triune
trivalent
trivial
triviality
trivially
trochaic

troche
troll
trolley
trombone
troop
troopship
trophy
tropic
tropical
tropically
trot
troth
trotter
troubadour
trouble
troublesome
troublingly
troublous
trough
trounce
troupe
trousers
trousseau
trout
trowel
truancy
truant
truce
truck
truckage
trucked

truckle
truckled
truckman
truculence
truculent
trudge
trudged
true
trueness
truffle
truism
truly
trump
trumped
trumpery
trumpet
trumpeter
trumpetweed
truncate
truncated
truncheon
trundle
trunk
trunnion
truss
trust
trustee
trusteeship
trustful
trustfully
trustfulness

trustworthiness
trustworthy
trusty
truth
truthful
truthfully
truthfulness
try
tryst
tub
tuba
tube
tuber
tubercle
tubercular
tuberculin
tuberculosis
tuberculous
tuberose
tubular
Tuesday
tuft
tug
tuition
tularemia
tulip
tulipwood
tulle
tumble
tumbler
tumor

tumult
tumultuous
tumultuously
tumulus
tun
tuna
tundra
tune
tuned
tuneful
tuneless
tuner
tungsten
tunic
tunnel
tunneled
tunny
turban
turbid
turbidity
turbidly
turbinate
turbine
turbot
turbulence
turbulent
turbulently
tureen
turf
turgid
turgidity
turgidly
Turk
turkey
turmeric
turmoil
turn
turnbuckle
turncoat
turned
turner
turnings
turnip
turnkey
turnout
turnover
turnpike
turnstile
turpentine
turpitude
turquoise
turret
turreted
turtle
Tuscan
tusk
tussle
tussled
tutelage
tutelary
tutor
tutored
tutorial
twain
twang
twanged
tweak
tweed
tweezers
twice
twiddle
twiddled
twig
twilight
twill
twin
twinborn
twine
twined
twinge
twinkle
twinkled
twirl
twirled
twist
twistings
twit
twitch
twitted
twitter
twittered
twitteringly
two

twofold
twosome
tycoon
type
typed
typesetter
typewriter
typewritten
typhoid
typhoon
typhous
typhus
typical
typification
typify
typist
typographer
typographic
typography
typothetae
tyrannical
tyrannicide
tyrannize
tyrannous
tyranny
tyrant
tyro

U

ubiquitous
udder
ugliness
ugly
ukase
ukulele
ulcer
ulcerate
ulceration
ulcerative
ulcerous
ulna
ulnar
ulster
ulterior
ultimate
ultimately
ultimatum
ultimo
ultramarine
ultramodern
ultraviolet
ululate
ululation
umber
umbrage
umbrella

umlaut
umpire
umpired
unable
unabridged
unaccented
unacceptable
unaccompanied
unaccountable
unaccustomed
unadjusted
unadorned
unadulterated
unaffected
unaided
unalloyed
unalterable
un-American
unamiable
unanimous
unanswerable
unappeasable
unapproachable
unappropriated
unarmed
unasked
unassailable

unassisted
unassuming
unattached
unattainable
unattempted
unattended
unauthenticated
unauthorized
unavailable
unavoidable
unaware
unbalanced
unballasted
unbar
unbecomingly
unbeknown
unbeknownst
unbelief
unbelievable
unbeliever
unbend
unbendingly
unbiased
unbidden
unbind
unblemished
unblushing

unbolted
unborn
unbosom
unbound
unbounded
unbowed
unbreakable
unbridled
unbuckle
unbuckled
unbusinesslike
unbutton
uncage
uncanny
unceasingly
unceremonious
unceremoniously
uncertain
uncertainly
uncertainty
unchallenged
unchangeable
uncharitable
unchecked
unchristened
unchristian
uncivil
uncivilized
unclad
unclaimed
unclasp

unclassified
uncle
unclean
uncleaned
unclosed
unclothed
uncoil
uncoiled
uncollectible
uncomfortable
uncomfortably
uncommon
uncommunicative
uncompanionable
uncomplimentary
uncompromising
unconcealed
unconcerned
unconditional
unconditionally
unconfined
uncongenial
unconquerable
unconquered
unconscionable
unconscious
unconsciously
unconsciousness
unconsidered
unconstitutional
uncontradicted

uncontrollable
unconventional
uncork
uncounted
uncouple
uncouth
uncover
uncovered
unction
unctuous
uncultivated
uncut
undamaged
undamped
undaunted
undeceive
undeceived
undecided
undecipherable
undeciphered
undefended
undefiled
undemonstrative
undeniable
under
underbid
underbrush
undercharge
underclothes
undercurrent
undercut

underdose
underestimate
underexpose
undergarment
underglaze
undergo
undergraduate
underground
undergrowth
underhanded
underlaid
underlie
underline
underling
undermine
underneath
underpaid
underpass
underpay
underpinning
underproduction
underrate
underscore
undersell
undershirt
undershot
undersigned
undersized
underskirt
underslung
understand
understandingly
understate
understatement
understood
understudy
undertake
undertaken
undertaker
undertone
undertook
undertow
undervalue
underwater
underwear
underwent
underworld
underwrite
underwriter
underwritten
undeserved
undesigned
undesired
undestroyed
undetermined
undeveloped
undigested
undignified
undimmed
undisciplined
undisclosed
undiscovered
undiscriminating
undisguised
undismayed
undisposed
undisputed
undistinguishable
undisturbed
undivided
undo
undone
undoubted
undress
undrinkable
undulant
undulate
undulation
undulous
undutiful
undying
unearned
unearth
unearthly
uneasiness
uneasy
uneatable
uneaten
uneducated
unembarrassed
unemployment
unencumbered
unendangered

unending
unendorsed
unendurable
unenforceable
unenterprising
unenvied
unequal
unequaled
unequally
unequipped
unequivocal
unerring
unessential
unestimated
unethical
uneven
uneventful
unexampled
unexcelled
unexceptionable
unexpected
unexpectedly
unexpectedness
unfaded
unfair
unfairly
unfairness
unfaithful
unfaithfulness
unfaltering
unfamiliar

unfashionable
unfasten
unfastened
unfavorable
unfeeling
unfeelingly
unfeigned
unfermented
unfettered
unfilled
unfinished
unfit
unflattering
unflinchingly
unfold
unforeseen
unforgettable
unforgivable
unformed
unfortified
unfortunate
unfortunately
unfrequented
unfriendly
unfruitful
unfunded
unfurl
unfurled
unfurnished
ungainly
ungodly

ungovernable
ungracious
ungrammatical
ungrateful
ungratefully
ungratefulness
ungrudgingly
unguarded
unguent
unguided
unhackneyed
unhampered
unhandy
unhanged
unhappiness
unhappy
unhardened
unharness
unhatched
unhealthful
unhealthy
unheard
unheeded
unheedful
unhesitatingly
unhinge
unhitch
unholy
unhonored
unhook
unhoped

unhorse
unhurt
unhygienic
unicorn
unidentified
unification
uniform
uniformed
uniformity
uniformly
unify
unilateral
unilluminated
unimaginable
unimaginative
unimpaired
unimpeachable
unimportant
unimpressionable
unimproved
unincorporated
uninformed
uninhabitable
uninhabited
uninitiated
uninjured
uninstructed
unintelligent
unintelligible
unintentional
unintentionally

uninterrupted
uninviting
union
unionism
unionist
unionization
unionize
unionized
unique
uniquely
uniqueness
unison
unissued
unit
Unitarian
unitary
unite
united
unity
universal
universality
universally
universe
university
unjustifiable
unkind
unkindliness
unknightly
unknowable
unknowingly
unknown

unlace
unladylike
unlatch
unlaundered
unlearn
unlearned
unleash
unleavened
unless
unlettered
unlicensed
unlike
unlikely
unlimited
unlisted
unlock
unlocked
unlooked
unlovable
unluckily
unlucky
unmake
unmanageable
unmanly
unmannerly
unmarried
unmask
unmatched
unmentionable
unmerciful
unmercifully

unmindful	unpopular	unrepentant
unmistakable	unpracticed	unreproved
unmixed	unprecedented	unrequited
unmolested	unprejudiced	unreserved
unmounted	unpremeditated	unreservedly
unnamed	unprepared	unresisting
unnatural	unpreparedness	unrestrained
unnecessary	unprepossessing	unrestricted
unnerve	unpretentious	unrewarded
unnumbered	unprincipled	unrighteous
unobjectionable	unprofessional	unripe
unobservant	unprogressive	unrivaled
unobserved	unpromising	unroll
unobtainable	unproved	unruffled
unoccupied	unpublished	unruly
unopened	unpunctual	unsaddle
unopposed	unqualified	unsafe
unorganized	unquestionable	unsaid
unpack	unquestionably	unsalable
unpaid	unquestioned	unsanctified
unpalatable	unreasonable	unsatisfactory
unparalleled	unreasonably	unsatisfied
unpardonable	unrebuked	unsavory
unpardoned	unrecognizable	unscrew
unparliamentary	unrecognized	unscrewed
unpaved	unreconciled	unscrupulous
unperturbed	unredeemed	unseasonable
unpleasant	unrelated	unseasoned
unplowed	unremitting	unseemly
unpolished	unremunerative	unseen
unpolluted	unrepaired	unselfish

unselfishly
unsettle
unsettled
unshakable
unshaven
unsheathe
unsheltered
unship
unshorn
unsightly
unsigned
unskilled
unskillful
unsmirched
unsnarl
unsociable
unsoiled
unsoldierly
unsolicited
unsophisticated
unsought
unsound
unspeakable
unspoken
unsportsmanlike
unstable
unstained
unsteadily
unsteady
unstrung
unsubstantial

unsubstantiated
unsuccessful
unsuitable
unsung
unsure
unsuspected
unsweetened
unswerving
unsympathetic
unsystematic
untangle
untangled
untainted
unteachable
untechnical
untenanted
untested
unthinkable
unthinking
unthinkingly
untidily
untidy
untie
until
untiringly
unto
untold
untouched
untoward
untracked
untranslatable

untried
untroubled
untrue
untruth
untruthful
untutored
untwine
untwist
unusable
unused
unusual
unusually
unutterable
unuttered
unvalued
unvarnished
unvarying
unveil
unversed
unwarrantable
unwarranted
unwary
unwarily
unwashed
unwaveringly
unwearied
unwelcome
unwell
unwholesome
unwieldy
unwilling

unwillingly
unwillingness
unwind
unwise
unwittingly
unwonted
unworkable
unworldly
unworthy
unwrap
unwreathe
unwritten
up
upas
upbraid
upgrowth
upheaval
upheld
uphill
uphold
upholder
upholster
upholsterer
upholstery
upkeep
uplift
upmost
upon
upper
uppermost
upright

uprising
uproar
uproarious
uproot
upset
upshot
upside
upstairs
upstart
uptake
uptown
upturn
upturned
upward
uranium
urban
urbane
urbanely
urbanity
urchin
urge
urged
urgency
urgent
urgently
urn
usable
usage
use
useful
usefully

usefulness
useless
uselessly
uselessness
user
uses
usher
usual
usually
usufruct
usurer
usurious
usurp
usurper
usury
utensil
utilitarian
utilitarianism
utilities
utility
utilizable
utilization
utilize
utilized
utmost
Utopia
Utopian
utter
utterance
uttered
utterly

V

vacancy
vacant
vacate
vacation
vacationist
vaccinate
vaccination
vaccine
vacillate
vacillatingly
vacillation
vacuity
vacuous
vacuum
vagabond
vagary
vagrancy
vagrant
vague
vagus
vain
vainglorious
vainglory
vainly
vainness
valance
valedictorian
valedictory
valence
valentine
valerian
valet
valiant
valid
validate
validated
validation
validity
validly
valise
valley
valor
valorous
valuable
valuation
value
valued
valueless
valve
valvular
valvulitis
vampire
vanadium
vandal
vandalism
vane
vanguard
vanilla
vanish
vanity
vanquish
vantage
vapid
vapidly
vapor
vaporization
vaporize
vaporized
vaporizer
vaporous
variability
variable
variance
variant
variation
varicose
varicosity
varied
variegate
variegation
variety

variola
various
variously
varnish
vary
vascular
vase
vaseline
vassal
vassalage
vast
vat
Vatican
vaudeville
vault
vaulted
vector
vedette
veer
veered
vegetable
vegetarian
vegetarianism
vegetate
vegetated
vegetation
vegetative
vehemence
vehement
vehemently
vehicle

vehicular
veil
veiled
vein
veined
veinlet
vellum
velocipede
velocity
velure
velvet
velveteen
velvety
venal
venality
vend
vendee
vender
vendible
vendor
veneer
venerable
venerate
venerated
veneration
vengeance
vengeful
venial
venially
venison
venom

venomously
ventilate
ventilation
ventilator
ventral
ventricle
ventricular
venture
ventured
venturesome
venue
veracious
veracity
veranda
verb
verbal
verbalization
verbalize
verbalized
verbally
verbatim
verbiage
verbose
verbosity
verdant
verdict
verdigris
verdure
verge
verged
verification

verify
verily
verisimilitude
veritable
veritably
verity
vermicelli
vermicide
vermiform
vermifuge
vermilion
vermin
verminous
vernacular
vernal
vernier
versatile
versatility
verse
versification
versifier
versify
version
verso
versus
vertebra
vertebrae
vertebrate
vertex
vertical
vertically

vertigo
verve
very
vesicle
vesper
vessel
vest
vestal
vested
vestibular
vestibule
vestige
vestigial
vestment
vestry
veteran
veterinarian
veterinary
veto
vex
vexation
vexatious
vexed
viability
viable
viaduct
vial
viand
vibrancy
vibrant
vibrate

vibrated
vibration
vibrator
vibratory
vicar
vicarage
vicarious
vicariously
vice
viceregal
viceroy
vicinity
vicious
viciously
vicissitude
victim
victimize
victimized
victor
Victorian
victorious
victoriously
victory
victual
victualed
video
vie
vied
view
viewed
vigil

vigilance
vigilant
vigilantly
vignette
vigor
vigorous
vigorously
vile
viler
vilest
vilification
vilify
villa
village
villager
vinaigrette
vinculum
vindicable
vindicate
vindication
vindictive
vine
vinegar
vineyard
vintage
vinylite
viol
violate
violated
violation
violative

violator
violence
violent
violently
violet
violets
violin
violinist
viper
virago
vireo
virgin
virginal
virginity
virile
virility
virtual
virtually
virtue
virtuosity
virtuoso
virtuous
virulence
virulency
virulent
virus
visa
visage
viscera
visceral
viscid

viscidity
viscose
viscosity
viscount
viscous
vise
visibility
visible
vision
visionary
visit
visitation
visited
visitor
vista
visual
visualization
visualize
visualized
visually
vital
vitality
vitalize
vitalized
vitally
vitamin
vitiate
vitiated
vitiation
vitreous
vitrification

vitrify
vitriol
vituperate
vituperation
vituperative
vivacious
vivaciously
vivacity
vivid
vividly
vivisection
vixen
vocabulary
vocal
vocalism
vocalist
vocalization
vocalize
vocalized
vocally
vocation
vocationally
vocative
vociferous
vodka
vogue
voice
voiced
voiceless
void
voidable

voided
volatile
volatility
volatilization
volatilize
volcanic
volcano
volition
volitional
volley
volt
voltage
voltameter
voltammeter
voltmeter
volubility
voluble
volubly
volume
volumetric
voluminous
voluntarily
voluntary
volunteer
voluptuary
voluptuous
voluptuously
volute
volvulus
vomica
vomit

vomited
vomitory
voodoo
voracious
voracity
vortex
vortical
votary
vote
voter
votive
vouch
vouched
voucher
vouchsafe
vow
vowed
vowel
voyage
vulcanization
vulcanize
vulgar
vulgarian
vulgarism
vulgarity
vulgarize
vulgarized
vulgarly
vulnerability
vulnerable
vulture

W

wad
waddle
wade
waded
wader
wafer
waffle
waft
wag
wage
waged
wager
wagered
waggle
waggled
wagon
waif
wail
wailed
wailings
wainscot
waist
waistband
waistline
wait
waited
waiter

waitress
waive
waiver
wake
wakeful
wakefully
wakefulness
waken
wale
walk
walker
walkout
walkover
wall
walled
wallet
wallets
wallflower
wallow
wallpaper
walnut
walrus
waltz
wampum
wan
wand
wander

wandered
wanderer
wane
waned
wangle
want
wanted
war
warble
warbler
ward
warded
warden
warder
wardrobe
wardroom
warehouse
warfare
warily
wariness
warlike
warm
warmed
warmly
warmth
warn
warned

warningly
warp
warrant
warranted
warrantor
warranty
warren
warship
wart
wary
was
wash
washable
washcloth
washer
washout
washroom
washstand
washwoman
wasp
waspish
wassail
wastage
waste
wastebasket
wasted
wasteful
wastefully
wastefulness
wastrel
watch

watchcase
watchdog
watchful
watchfully
watchfulness
watchmaker
watchman
watchtower
watchword
water
watered
waterfall
waterfowl
waterlogged
Waterloo
watermark
waterproof
watershed
waterside
waterspout
waterway
waterworks
watery
watt
wattage
wattle
wattled
wattmeter
wave
waver
wavered

waveringly
waviness
wavy
wax
waxen
waxiness
waxwing
waxy
way
waybill
wayfarer
waylaid
waylay
wayside
wayward
waywardness
we
weak
weaken
weakened
weaker
weakest
weakling
weakly
weakness
wealth
wealthier
wealthiest
wealthy
weapon
wear

wearable
wearer
wearily
weariness
wearings
weary
weasel
weather
weatherboard
weathercock
weathered
weatherproof
weave
weaver
web
webbing
wed
wedded
wedding
wedge
wedged
wedlock
Wednesday
weed
weedy
week
weekday
weekly
weep
weevil
weft
weigh
weighings
weight
weighty
weir
weird
weirdly
weirdness
welcome
welcomed
weld
welded
welfare
well
welt
welter
weltered
wen
wench
wend
wended
went
wept
were
west
westerly
western
westerner
westward
wet
wetness
whack
whale
whaleback
whalebone
whaler
wharf
wharfage
wharfinger
what
whatever
whatnot
whatsoever
wheat
wheaten
wheatworm
wheedle
wheedled
wheel
wheelbarrow
wheeled
wheelwright
wheeze
whelk
whelp
when
whence
whenever
whensoever
where
whereabouts
whereas

whereat
whereby
wherefore
wherefrom
wherein
whereof
whereon
wheresoever
whereupon
wherever
wherewith
wherewithal
wherry
whet
whetted
whether
which
whichever
whichsoever
whiff
Whig
while
whilom
whim
whimper
whimpered
whimsey
whimsical
whimsically
whine
whined
whip
whipcord
whippet
whipstitch
whipstock
whipworm
whir
whirl
whirled
whirligig
whirlpool
whirlwind
whisk
whisker
whisky
whisper
whispered
whisperer
whist
whistle
whistled
white
whitecap
whitefish
whiten
whiteness
whitewash
whitewings
whitewood
whither
whitlow
whittle
whittled
who
whoever
whole
wholehearted
wholesale
wholesaler
wholesome
wholesomely
wholly
whoop
whose
whosoever
why
wick
wicked
wickedness
wicker
wickerwork
wicket
wide
widen
wider
widespread
widest
widow
widowed
widower
widowhood
width

wield
wife
wig
wiggle
wiggled
wigwag
wigwam
wild
wilderness
wildfire
wildness
wile
will
willed
willful
willfully
willfulness
willingly
willingness
willow
wily
win
wince
winch
wind
windage
windbreak
windfall
windily
windings
windjammer

windlass
windmill
window
windowpane
windpipe
windrow
windstorm
windward
windy
wine
wineglass
wing
winged
wingless
wink
winked
winkle
winner
winningly
winnings
winnow
winsome
winter
wipe
wiper
wire
wired
wireless
wirepulling
wireworm
wisdom

wise
wiseacre
wisely
wiser
wisest
wish
wished
wishful
wishfully
wisp
wistful
wistfully
wistfulness
wit
witch
witchcraft
witchery
with
withal
withdraw
withdrawal
withdrew
wither
withered
witheringly
withhold
within
without
withstand
witless
witness

witticism
wittingly
witty
wives
wizard
wizardly
wizardry
wizened
woe
woebegone
woeful
woefully
wolf
wolfhound
wolfish
wolverene
wolves
woman
womanhood
womankind
womanlike
womanliness
womanly
women
won
wonder
wonderful
wonderfully
wonderingly
wonderland
wonderment

wonderwork
wondrous
wondrously
won't
wont
woo
wood
woodchuck
wooded
wooden
woodland
woodman
woodpecker
woodsman
woodwork
woodworm
wooer
woof
wool
woolen
wooliness
woolly
word
wordiness
wordy
work
workable
worked
worker
workhouse
workings

workman
workmanship
workmen
workshop
workwoman
workwomen
world
worldliness
worldly
worm
wormwood
wormy
worn
worried
worrier
worriment
worrisome
worry
worse
worship
worshiped
worshiper
worshipful
worst
worsted
worsted
worth
worthily
worthiness
worthless
worthy

would	wrecker	writ
wound	wren	write
wound	wrench	writer
wove	wrest	writhe
woven	wrestle	writings
wrack	wrestled	written
wraith	wrestler	wrong
wrangle	wretch	wrongful
wrangled	wretchedly	wrongfully
wrap	wretchedness	wrongheaded
wrapper	wriggle	wrongly
wrappings	wriggled	wrongness
wrath	wring	wrote
wrathful	wringer	wroth
wrathfully	wrinkle	wrought
wreath	wrinkled	wrung
wreck	wrist	wry
wreckage	wristlet	wryneck

X Y Z

xenon
xeroderma
xerosis
X-ray
xylophone
xyster

yacht
yachtsman
yak
Yale
yam
yank
Yankee
yard
yardage
yardarm
yardstick
yarn
yarrow
yaw
yawl
yawn
ye
yea
year
yearbook
yearling
yearly
yearn
yearningly
yearnings
yeast
yeasty
yell
yelled
yellow
yelp
yeoman
yeomanry
yes
yesterday
yet
yew
yield
yielded
yieldingly
yodel
yoga
yolk
yon
yonder
yore
you
young
younger
youngest
youngish
youngster
your
yourself
yourselves
youthful
youthfully
youthfulness
ytterbium
yttrium
yucca
yule
yuletide

zany
zeal
zealot
zealotry
zealously
zebra
zebu
zenith
zephyr
Zeppelin

zero	Zionism	zone
zest	Zionist	zoo
zigzag	zipper	zoological
zinc	zirconium	Zulu
Zion	zodiac	zymology

PART TWO

PERSONAL AND GEOGRAPHICAL NAMES

Part Two consists of 2,604 entries of personal and geographical names divided approximately as follows:

1,600 geographical names. The largest group of names consists of the names of American cities and towns that are likely to be encountered in business dictation. The names of the American states and territories are given. A relatively small group of foreign geographical names is given—the foreign countries and cities that are most likely to occur in American business dictation. The lists are not intended to be complete or exhaustive. The attempt has been made, however, to include the geographical names that occur most frequently in ordinary business dictation.

350 surnames. This small group of last names represents the commonest American last names that are likely to be used in business dictation. There are tens of thousands of surnames in this country, and no attempt can be made to present a complete list.

350 first names of women. This list contains the more frequently used feminine first names.

350 first names of men. This list contains the more frequently used masculine first names.

The four groups of names listed above are combined in one alphabetical list in Part Two.

With the exception of the states and of a few of the largest cities, the geographical names are written very fully. This is done with the understanding that the writer will use these full outlines for the names that occur only occasionally in the dictation. When some name occurs more frequently in the dictation, an abbreviated form will be used.

The shorthand writer in Oregon would ordinarily have little occasion to use the outline for *Corpus Christi*. The Texan shorthand writer might use it so frequently that he would abbreviate it to *kk*.

In order to keep the list in Part Two as short and at the same time as useful as possible the names of many cities and towns are omitted. This is possible because many American city and town names are composed of nouns and adjectives that appear in Part One—such names as *White River Junction* or *Egg Harbor City*.

Many cities and towns form their names by adding to the name of another town a word like *Beach, Grove, Hill, City, Park,* or *Spring*. In most cases such names have been omitted as they would cause no shorthand writing difficulty.

PERSONAL AND GEOGRAPHICAL NAMES

Aaron
Abbott
Abel
Aberdeen
Abigail
Abilene
Abington
Abner
Abraham
Abram
Ada
Adam
Adams
Adelaide
Adelbert
Adler
Adolph
Adrian
Adrienne
Afghanistan
Africa
Agatha
Agnes
Aiken
Aileen
Ainsworth
Akron

Alabama
Alameda
Alamosa
Alan
Alaska
Albania
Albany
Albert
Alberta
Albia
Albion
Albuquerque
Alcoa
Alexander
Alexandra
Alexandria
Alexis
Alfred
Algeria
Algernon
Alhambra
Alice
Alicia
Aliquippa
Allan
Allen
Allentown

Alliance
Allison
Alma
Alonso
Alpena
Alphonsine
Alphonso
Althea
Alton
Altoona
Altus
Alva
Alvin
Amanda
Amarillo
Ambridge
Ambrose
Amelia
Americus
Ames
Amesbury
Amherst
Amityville
Amos
Amsterdam
Amy
Anaconda

Anacortes
Anaheim
Anastasia
Andalusia
Anderson
Andover
Andrews
Angela
Angelica
Angora
Angus
Anita
Ann
Anna
Annabel
Annapolis
Ann Arbor
Annette
Anniston
Anoka
Anselm
Ansonia
Anthony
Antigo
Antioch
Antoinette
Antonia
Antwerp
Appleton
Arabella
Arabia
Arcadia
Archer
Archibald
Ardmore
Argentina
Arizona
Arkadelphia
Arkansas
Arline
Arlington
Armstrong
Arnold
Arthur
Asa
Asbury Park
Asheboro
Asheville
Ashland
Ashley
Ashtabula
Astoria
Asunción
Atchison
Athelstan
Athena
Athens
Athol
Atkinson
Atlanta
Atlantic
Atlantic City
Attleboro
Aubrey
Auckland
Audry
Audubon
Augusta
Augustin
Aurelia
Aurelius
Aurora
Austin
Australia
Austria
Avalon
Avery
Avis
Ayres
Azusa
Bacon
Bailey
Bainbridge
Baird
Baker
Bakersfield
Baldwin
Ballard
Baltimore
Bangkok
Bangor
Baptist
Baptista

Baraboo	Beacon	Benedicta
Barbara	Beale	Bender
Barberton	Beardstown	Benjamin
Barcelona	Beatrice	Bennett
Barlow	Beaumont	Bennington
Barnabas	Beaver	Benson
Barnaby	Beaver Dam	Bentley
Barnard	Beaver Falls	Benton
Barnesville	Becker	Benton Harbor
Barnett	Beckley	Berea
Barnstable	Bedford	Bergenfield
Barranquilla	Beecher	Berkeley
Bartholomew	Belfast	Berlin
Barre	Belgium	Bernard
Barrett	Belinda	Bernstein
Barrington	Bell	Bertha
Bartlesville	Bella	Bertram
Bartlett	Bellaire	Bertrand
Bartow	Belle	Berwick
Basil	Bellefontaine	Berwyn
Bastrop	Bellefonte	Beryl
Batavia	Belleville	Bessemer
Batesville	Bellevue	Bessie
Bath	Bellingham	Bethlehem
Baton Rouge	Bellwood	Beulah
Battle Creek	Belmont	Beverly
Bauer	Beloit	Bicknell
Baxter	Belvedere	Biddeford
Bayard	Bemidji	Big Spring
Bay City	Bend	Billings
Bayonne	Benedict	Biloxi

Binghamton
Birmingham
Bisbee
Bishop
Bismarck
Bissell
Blackstone
Blackwell
Blair
Blairsville
Blake
Blakely
Blanchard
Blanche
Bliss
Bloomfield
Bloomington
Bloomsburg
Bluefield
Blue Island
Bluffton
Blytheville
Bogalusa
Bogota
Boise
Bolivia
Bombay
Bonham
Boniface
Boone
Boonton

Boonville
Bordeaux
Boris
Boston
Bosworth
Boulder
Bound Brook
Bowen
Bowling Green
Bowman
Boyd
Boyle
Bozeman
Brackenridge
Braddock
Bradenton
Bradford
Bradley
Brady
Brainerd
Braintree
Brattleboro
Brawley
Brazil
Bremen
Bremerton
Brenham
Brennan
Brentwood
Brewer
Brewster

Brian
Bridgeport
Bridget
Bridgeton
Bridgewater
Briggs
Brigham
Brisbane
Bristol
Bristow
Brockton
Bronxville
Brookfield
Brookhaven
Brookings
Brown
Brownsville
Brownwood
Bruce
Bruno
Brunswick
Brussels
Bryan
Bryant
Bucharest
Bucyrus
Budapest
Buenos Aires
Buffalo
Bulgaria
Burbank

Burke	Camilla	Cartersville
Burley	Campbell	Carthage
Burlingame	Campeche	Casper
Burlington	Canada	Catharine
Burma	Canal Zone	Cathleen
Burns	Canfield	Catskill
Burrillville	Cannon	Cecelia
Burroughs	Canon City	Cecil
Burton	Canonsburg	Cedar Falls
Butler	Canton	Cedarhurst
Butte	Cape Girardeau	Cedar Rapids
Byron	Cape Town	Cedartown
Cable	Caracas	Cedric
Cadillac	Carbondale	Celeste
Cadwallader	Carey	Celestine
Caesar	Carlisle	Celia
Cairo	Carlotta	Centerville
Calais	Carlsbad	Central Falls
Calcutta	Carlson	Centralia
Caldwell	Carlstadt	Ceylon
Caleb	Carlton	Chalmers
Calexico	Carmel	Chambersburg
Calgary	Carmen	Champaign
Calhoun	Carnegie	Chandler
California	Carol	Chanute
Callahan	Carpenter	Chapman
Calumet City	Carroll	Chariton
Calvin	Carrollton	Charleroi
Cambridge	Carson	Charles
Camden	Carter	Charleston
Cameron	Carteret	Charlotte

Charlottesville	Cicely	Clifton Forge
Chase	Cicero	Clinton
Chattanooga	Cincinnati	Cloquet
Chauncy	Circleville	Clotilda
Cheboygan	Clairton	Clovis
Chelsea	Clara	Coaldale
Cheltenham	Clare	Coatesville
Cherbourg	Claremont	Cobb
Cherokee	Clarence	Coddington
Chester	Claribel	Coeur d'Alene
Cheviot	Clarice	Coffeyville
Cheyenne	Clarinda	Cohen
Chicago	Clark	Cohoes
Chickasha	Clarksburg	Colby
Chico	Clarksdale	Coldwater
Chicopee	Clarksville	Coleman
Chihuahua	Claudia	College Park
Childress	Claudius	Collier
Childs	Claudine	Collingdale
Chile	Clayton	Collingswood
Chillicothe	Clearfield	Collins
China	Clearwater	Collinsville
Chippewa Falls	Cleary	Cologne
Chisholm	Cleburne	Colombia
Christabel	Clement	Colorado
Christchurch	Clementina	Colorado Springs
Christian	Clementine	Colton
Christina	Cleveland	Columbia
Christine	Clifford	Columbia Heights
Christopher	Cliffside Park	Columbus
Chula Vista	Clifton	Compton

Comstock	Corinna	Cudahy
Concord	Corinth	Culbertson
Concordia	Cork	Cullman
Condon	Cornelia	Culver City
Cone	Cornelius	Cumberland
Conklin	Corning	Cummings
Conley	Corona	Cummins
Connecticut	Coronado	Curtis
Connellsville	Corpus Christi	Cushing
Connelly	Corry	Cuthbert
Connersville	Corsicana	Cutler
Connolly	Cortland	Cynthia
Connor	Corvallis	Cyril
Conrad	Corwin	Cyrus
Conshohocken	Coshocton	Czechoslovakia
Constance	Costa Rica	Dagmar
Constant	Council Bluffs	Dallas
Constantine	Covington	Dalton
Constantinople	Crafton	Daly
Conway	Craig	Dan
Cook	Crandall	Danbury
Cooley	Cranford	Daniel
Coolidge	Cranston	Daphne
Cooper	Crawford	Davenport
Copenhagen	Crawfordsville	Danville
Cora	Creston	Darby
Coral Gables	Crispin	Darlington
Coraopolis	Cromwell	Dartmouth
Corbin	Crookston	David
Cordele	Crowley	Davidson
Cordelia	Cuba	Davis

Dawson
Dayton
Daytona Beach
Dean
Dearborn
Deborah
Decatur
Decker
Decorah
Dedham
Deerfield
Defiance
De Kalb
De Land
Delaware
Delhi
Delia
Della
Delphine
Delphos
Del Rio
Demetrius
Denise
Denison
Denmark
Dennison
Denton
Denver
De Pere
Depew
Derby

Des Moines
De Soto
Detroit
Devils Lake
Dewey
Dexter
Diana
Dick
Dickinson
Dickson City
Dillon
Dinah
District of Columbia
Dix
Dixon
Dobbs Ferry
Dodge City
Dolores
Dominic
Dominican Republic
Donald
Donora
Donovan
Dora
Dorcas
Doris
Dormont
Dorothea
Dorothy
Dougherty
Douglas

Dover
Dowagiac
Downers Grove
Doyle
Dresden
Driscoll
Drusilla
Dublin
Du Bois
Dubuque
Dudley
Duffy
Dulcie
Duluth
Dumont
Dunbar
Duncan
Dunn
Dunellen
Dunkirk
Dunmore
Duquesne
Durango
Durant
Durham
Duryea
Dwight
Dyersburg
Eagle Pass
Earl
Easley

East Aurora	Effingham	Eloise
East Chicago	Egan	El Paso
Easthampton	Egbert	El Reno
East Hartford	Egypt	Elsa
East Lansing	Eileen	El Salvador
Eastman	Eire	Elsie
East Moline	Elaine	Elspeth
Easton	Elbert	Elton
East Orange	Elberton	Elvira
East Peoria	Eldred	Elwood
East Pittsburgh	El Centro	Ely
East Point	El Cerrito	Elyria
East Providence	Eleanor	Emery
East Rochester	Electra	Emil
East Rutherford	Elgin	Emily
East Stroudsburg	Elihu	Emma
Eau Claire	Elijah	Emmanuel
Ebenezer	Elisha	Emporia
Ecuador	Elizabeth	Endicott
Edgar	Elizabethton	England
Edina	Elk City	Englewood
Edinburgh	Elkhart	Enid
Edith	Elkins	Ennis
Edmonton	Ellen	Enos
Edmund	Ellensburg	Enrico
Edna	Elliott	Enright
Edward	Ellsworth	Ephraim
Edwardsville	Ellwood City	Ephrata
Edwin	Elmer	Erasmus
Edwina	Elmhurst	Erastus
Effie	Elmira	Eric

Erie
Erma
Ernest
Ernestine
Erwin
Escanaba
Estella
Esther
Estherville
Esthonia
Ethan
Ethel
Ethiopia
Etna
Etta
Euclid
Eudora
Eugene
Eugenia
Eulalia
Eunice
Euphemia
Eureka
Europe
Eustace
Eva
Evangeline
Evanston
Evansville
Eve
Eveleth

Evelina
Evelyn
Everard
Everett
Exeter
Ezra
Fairbanks
Fairbury
Fairfield
Fairhaven
Fairlawn
Fairmont
Fairview
Faith
Fall River
Falls City
Fargo
Farrell
Fayetteville
Feldman
Felix
Ferdinand
Fergus Falls
Ferguson
Ferndale
Fidelia
Field
Findlay
Finland
Finley
Fisher

Fitchburg
Fitzgerald
Flagstaff
Flat River
Flavia
Fleming
Flint
Flora
Florence
Florida
Floyd
Flynn
Foley
Fond du Lac
Ford
Ford City
Forest City
Forest Park
Forest Hills
Fort Atkinson
Fort Collins
Fort Dodge
Fort Lauderdale
Fort Lee
Fort Madison
Fort Myers
Fort Pierce
Fort Scott
Fort Smith
Fort Thomas
Fort Wayne

Fort Worth
Foster
Fostoria
Fox
Framingham
France
Frances
Francis
Frankfort
Franklin
Fraser
Frederic
Frederica
Fredericksburg
Fredericton
Freehold
Freeland
Freeman
Freeport
Fremont
French
Fredonia
Fresno
Frieda
Frostburg
Fuller
Fullerton
Fulton
Gabriel
Gabriella
Gadsden

Gaffney
Gail
Gainesville
Galesburg
Galion
Gallagher
Gallup
Galveston
Garden City
Gardiner
Gardner
Garfield
Garret
Gary
Gasper
Gastonia
Geneva
Genevieve
Genoa
Geoffrey
George
Georgetown
Georgia
Gerald
Geraldine
Gerard
Germany
Gertrude
Gettysburg
Gibson
Gideon

Gifford
Gilbert
Girard
Gladys
Glasgow
Glassport
Gleason
Glencoe
Glen Cove
Glendale
Glenn
Glenna
Glen Ridge
Glen Rock
Glens Falls
Globe
Gloria
Gloucester
Gloversville
Goddard
Godfrey
Goldberg
Goldsboro
Goodwin
Gordon
Goshen
Gould
Grace
Grafton
Graham
Grand Forks

Grand Haven
Grand Island
Grand Junction
Grand Rapids
Grant
Grants Pass
Graves
Gray
Great Barrington
Great Britain
Great Falls
Great Neck
Greece
Greeley
Green
Green Bay
Greenfield
Greensboro
Greensburg
Greenville
Greenwood
Gregory
Grenada
Greta
Gretchen
Gretna
Griffin
Griffiths
Grinnell
Griselda
Gross

Grosse Pointe
Grove City
Grover
Guadalajara
Guam
Guatemala
Gulfport
Gustavus
Gutenberg
Guthrie
Guy
Hackensack
Haddonfield
Haddon Heights
Hagerstown
Haggerty
Haiti
Halifax
Hall
Hamburg
Hamilton
Hammond
Hampton
Hancock
Hanford
Hannah
Hannibal
Hanover
Hans
Hansen
Hanson

Harding
Harlan
Harley
Harold
Harper
Harriet
Harriman
Harrington
Harris
Harrisburg
Harrison
Harrisonburg
Hartford
Hartman
Hartsville
Harvey
Hasbrouck Heights
Hastings
Hattiesburg
Havana
Haverford
Haverstraw
Havre
Hawaii
Hawthorne
Hays
Hayward
Hazard
Healy
Hector
Hedwig

Helen
Helena
Heloise
Hempstead
Henderson
Henrietta
Henry
Herbert
Herkimer
Herman
Hermosa Beach
Herrin
Hester
Hezekiah
Hibbing
Hickory
Higgins
Highland Park
High Point
Hilda
Hill
Hillsboro
Hillsdale
Hillside
Hingham
Hinsdale
Hinton
Hiram
Hobart
Hoboken
Hodges

Hoffman
Holdenville
Holland
Hollywood
Holmes
Holt
Holyoke
Homer
Homestead
Homewood
Honduras
Honesdale
Hong Kong
Honolulu
Hoover
Hope
Hopewell
Hopkins
Hopkinsville
Horace
Horatio
Hornel
Hortense
Horton
Hosea
Hot Springs
Houston
Howard
Howell
Hubbs
Hubert

Hudson
Hugh
Hughes
Hugo
Huldah
Humboldt
Humphrey
Hungary
Hunter
Huntington
Huntsville
Huron
Hutchinson
Hyattsville
Iceland
Ichabod
Ida
Idaho
Idaho Falls
Ignatius
Illinois
Imogene
Independence
India
Indiana
Indianapolis
Inglewood
Iola
Iowa
Iowa City
Ipswich

Ira
Iran
Iraq
Ireland
Irene
Iris
Irma
Iron Mountain
Ironton
Ironwood
Irving
Irvington
Irwin
Isaac
Isabel
Isadora
Ishpeming
Isidore
Isolde
Israel
Istanbul
Italy
Ithaca
Ivan
Ivy
Jabez
Jack
Jackson
Jacksonville
Jacobs
Jacqueline
Jamaica
James
Jamestown
Jane
Janesville
Janet
Janice
Japan
Jared
Jarvis
Jason
Jasper
Jean
Jeannette
Jefferson
Jeffersonville
Jeffrey
Jemima
Jenkins
Jenkintown
Jennifer
Jennings
Jenny
Jeremiah
Jerome
Jersey City
Jerusalem
Jessamine
Jesse
Jessica
Jessie
Joan
Job
Jocelin
Jock
Joel
John
Johnson
Johnston
Johnstown
Joliet
Jonah
Jonas
Jonathan
Jones
Jonesboro
Joplin
Joseph
Joyce
Judah
Jude
Judith
Julia
Julian
Juliana
Juliet
Julius
June
Junius
Justin
Justina
Kabul

Kalamazoo	Keyport	Lake City
Kalispell	Keyser	Lake Forest
Kane	Key West	Lakeland
Kankakee	Kharkov	Lake Wales
Kansas	Kilgore	Lakewood
Kansas City	Kimball	Lake Worth
Karen	King	Lambert
Karl	Kingsford	Lancaster
Kate	Kingston	Lancelot
Katharine	Kingsville	Lanett
Kathleen	Kinston	Lansdale
Kawanee	Kirksville	Lansdowne
Kearny	Kirkwood	Lansford
Keene	Kittanning	Lansing
Keith	Kitty	La Paz
Kelly	Klamath Falls	Lapeer
Kelso	Klein	La Porte
Kelvin	Knight	Laramie
Kendallville	Knox	Larchmont
Kenmore	Knoxville	Laredo
Kennedy	Kokomo	Larksville
Kenneth	Korea	Lars
Kennett	Laban	Larson
Kenosha	Lacey	La Salle
Kent	Lackawanna	Las Cruces
Kenton	Laconia	Las Vegas
Kentucky	La Crosse	Latrobe
Keokuk	La Grande	Latvia
Kerr	Lafayette	Laughlin
Kerrville	La Junta	Laura
Kester	Lake Charles	Laurel

Laurens
Laurinburg
Lavinia
Lawrence
Lawrenceville
Lawton
Lazarus
Lead
Leah
Leander
Leavenworth
Lebanon
Lederer
Lee
Leeds
Lehighton
Lehman
Leipsig
Lelia
Le Mars
Lemuel
Lena
Leningrad
Lenoir
Leo
Leominster
Leon
Leonard
Leonia
Leonora
Leopold

Leroy
Leslie
Lester
Letitia
Lettice
Levy
Lewis
Lewiston
Lewistown
Lexington
Libby
Liberia
Liechtenstein
Lillian
Lilly
Lima
Limon
Lincoln
Linden
Lindstrom
Linton
Lionel
Lisa
Lisbon
Litchfield
Lithuania
Little Falls
Little Rock
Liverpool
Livingston
Livingstone

Llewellyn
Lloyd
Lockhart
Lock Haven
Lockport
Lodi
Logan
Logansport
Lois
Lola
Lombard
London
Long
Long Beach
Long Branch
Longview
Lorain
Lorenzo
Loretta
Lorinda
Los Angeles
Louis
Louisa
Louise
Louisiana
Louisville
Loveland
Lowell
Lubbock
Lucinda
Lucius

Lucretia
Lucy
Ludington
Ludlow
Luella
Lufkin
Luke
Lumberton
Luther
Luxembourg
Luzerne
Lydia
Lyle
Lynbrook
Lynch
Lynchburg
Lyndhurst
Lynn
Lynwood
Lyons
Mabel
Mack
Madeline
Madge
Madison
Madisonville
Madrid
Mae
Magdalene
Maguire
Mahanoy City

Mahoney
Maine
Malden
Malone
Malvern
Malverne
Manchester
Mandan
Mandy
Manhattan
Manila
Manistee
Manistique
Manitoba
Manitowoc
Mankato
Mannheim
Manuel
Manzala
Maple Heights
Maplewood
Marblehead
Marcella
Marcellus
Marcia
Marcus
Margaret
Marguery
Marian
Marianna
Marietta

Marilla
Marinette
Marion
Marlboro
Marlin
Marquette
Marseilles
Marshall
Marshalltown
Marshfield
Martha
Martin
Martinez
Martinsburg
Martinsville
Maryville
Mason
Mason City
Massachusetts
Massena
Massillon
Mathilda
Matthew
Mattoon
Maud
Maurice
Maximilian
Maxwell
May
Maynard
Maysville

Mayville	Menominee	Minden
Maywood	Mercedes	Mineola
McAdoo	Mercy	Minersville
McCabe	Meriden	Minerva
McCann	Merrill	Mingo Junction
McCarthy	Mesa	Minneapolis
McCauley	Methuen	Minnesota
McComb	Metuchen	Minnie
McCook	Mexico	Minot
McCormack	Meyer	Miranda
McDonald	Miami	Miriam
McGregor	Micah	Mission
McIntosh	Michael	Mississippi
McKee	Michigan	Missoula
McKeesport	Middleboro	Missouri
McKees Rocks	Middletown	Mitchell
McKenzie	Midland	Moberly
McKinney	Milan	Mobile
McLean	Mildred	Modesto
McLeod	Miles	Moira
McMillan	Miles City	Moline
McPherson	Milford	Monaca
Meadville	Milicent	Monessen
Mechanicsburg	Millburn	Monica
Mechanicville	Millbury	Monmouth
Medford	Milledgeville	Monroe
Melbourne	Miller	Monrovia
Melissa	Millvale	Montague
Melrose	Millville	Montana
Memphis	Milton	Montclair
Menasha	Milwaukee	Montebello

Monterey
Montevideo
Montgomery
Montpelier
Montreal
Moore
Mooresville
Moorhead
Morgan
Morgantown
Morocco
Morris
Morrison
Morristown
Morrisville
Morse
Mortimer
Moscow
Moses
Moultrie
Moundsville
Mount Airy
Mount Carmel
Mount Clemens
Mount Kisco
Mount Lebanon
Mount Oliver
Mount Pleasant
Mount Vernon
Muncie
Munhall

Munich
Murdock
Murfreesboro
Muriel
Murphy
Murphysboro
Murray
Muscatine
Muskegon
Myers
Myra
Myrtle
Naaman
Nampa
Nancy
Nanking
Nannette
Nanticoke
Nanty-Glo
Naomi
Napa
Naperville
Naples
Napoleon
Nash
Nashua
Nashville
Natal
Natalie
Natchez
Natchitoches

Nathan
Nathaniel
Natick
Naugatuck
Nazareth
Neal
Nebraska
Needham
Neenah
Negaunee
Nehemiah
Nellie
Nelson
Nelsonville
Neptune
Nerissa
Netherlands
Nevada
New Albany
Newark
New Bedford
New Bern
Newberry
New Boston
New Braunfels
New Brighton
New Britain
New Brunswick
Newburgh
Newburyport
New Castle

Newfoundland	North Adams	Oelwein
New Hampshire	Northampton	Ogden
New Haven	North Bergen	Ogdensburg
New Jersey	North Braddock	Ohio
New Kensington	Northbridge	Oil City
New London	North Carolina	Oklahoma
New Mexico	North Chicago	Oklahoma City
New Orleans	North Dakota	Okmulgee
Newport	North Platte	Old Forge
Newport News	Norwalk	Old Town
New Rochelle	Norway	Olean
Newton	Norwich	Olga
New Ulm	Norwood	Olive
New York	Nottingham	Oliver
New Zealand	Nova Scotia	Olney
Niagara Falls	Nuremberg	Olsen
Nicaragua	Nutley	Olson
Nicholas	Nyack	Olympia
Niles	Oakland	Olyphant
Niles Center	Oakmont	Omaha
Nina	Oak Park	Oneida
Noah	Oakwood	O'Neil
Noel	Obadiah	Oneonta
Nogales	O'Brien	Ontario
Nolan	Ocala	Opelika
Nora	O'Connor	Opelousas
Norfolk	Oconto	Ophelia
Norma	Octavia	Orange
Normal	Octavius	Orangeburg
Norman	Odessa	Oregon
Norristown	O'Donnell	Orlando

Oscar	Parkersburg	Peoria
Oshkosh	Park Ridge	Percival
Oskaloosa	Parma	Percy
Oslo	Parsons	Perry
Osmund	Pasadena	Perth Amboy
Ossining	Pascagoula	Peru
Oswald	Passaic	Petaluma
Oswego	Patchogue	Peter
Ottawa	Paterson	Petersburg
Otto	Patience	Petersen
Ottumwa	Patricia	Peterson
Owego	Patrick	Petoskey
Owen	Paul	Phelps
Owensboro	Paula	Philadelphia
Owosso	Paulina	Philander
Oxnard	Pauline	Philip
Packard	Paulsboro	Philippa
Paducah	Pawtucket	Philippine Islands
Painesville	Peabody	Phillips
Palestine	Peale	Phillipsburg
Palmer	Pearl	Phineas
Palmerton	Pearson	Phoebe
Palmyra	Peekskill	Phoenix
Palo Alto	Peggy	Phoenixville
Pamela	Pekin	Phyllis
Pampa	Pelham	Piedmont
Panama	Pendleton	Pierce
Pansy	Penns Grove	Pine Bluff
Paraguay	Pennsylvania	Pitcairn
Paris	Penn Yan	Pitman
Parker	Pensacola	Pittsburgh

Pittsfield
Pittston
Pius
Plainfield
Plains
Plainview
Plant City
Plaquemine
Plattsburg
Pleasantville
Plymouth
Pocatello
Poland
Polly
Ponca City
Pontiac
Portage
Portales
Port Angeles
Port Arthur
Port Chester
Porter
Porterville
Port Huron
Portia
Port Jervis
Portland
Portsmouth
Portugal
Potter
Pottstown

Pottsville
Poughkeepsie
Powell
Powers
Prague
Pratt
Prescott
Presque Isle
Price
Prichard
Princeton
Priscilla
Providence
Provo
Prudence
Pueblo
Puerto Rico
Pulaski
Putnam
Puyallup
Quakertown
Quebec
Queensland
Quincy
Quinn
Quito
Rachel
Racine
Radford
Rahway
Raleigh

Ralph
Ramona
Randall
Randolph
Rankin
Rapid City
Raton
Ravenna
Ray
Raymond
Reading
Reba
Rebecca
Red Bank
Redlands
Red Oak
Red Wing
Redwood City
Regina
Reginald
Reid
Reidsville
Reinhardt
Reno
Renshaw
Rensselaer
Reuben
Revere
Rex
Reynolds
Rhea

Rhinelander
Rhoda
Rhode Island
Rhodes
Richard
Richfield
Richman
Richmond
Richwood
Ridgefield
Ridgeway
Ridgewood
Riga
Riley
Rio de Janeiro
Rita
River Rouge
Riverside
Roanoke
Robbins
Robbinsdale
Robert
Robertson
Robinson
Robstown
Rochester
Rockford
Rock Island
Rockland
Rock Springs
Rockville

Rocky Mount
Roderick
Roger
Roland
Rolla
Rollo
Romania
Rome
Romola
Roosevelt
Rosa
Rosalind
Roscoe
Roselle
Rosemary
Roseville
Ross
Rossville
Roswell
Rotterdam
Rowena
Roy
Royal Oak
Ruby
Rudolph
Rufus
Rumford Falls
Rupert
Rushville
Rusk
Russell

Russia
Ruston
Ruth
Rutherford
Rutland
Ryan
Rye
Ryerson
Saco
Sacramento
Saginaw
Saguenay
St. Albans
St. Augustine
St. Bernard
St. Charles
St. Clair
St. Cloud
St. John
St. Johnsbury
St. Joseph
St. Louis
St. Marys
St. Paul
St. Peter
St. Petersburg
Salamanca
Salem
Salina
Salinas
Salisbury

Salome
Salt Lake City
Sampson
Samuel
San Angelo
San Anselmo
San Antonio
San Benito
San Bernardino
San Bruno
Sanders
San Diego
Sand Springs
Sandusky
San Fernando
Sanford
San Francisco
San Gabriel
San Jose
San Leandro
San Luis Obispo
San Marcos
San Marino
San Mateo
San Rafael
Santa Ana
Santa Barbara
Santa Clara
Santa Cruz
Santa Fe
Santa Maria

Santa Monica
Santa Paula
Santa Rosa
Santiago
Sapulpa
Sarah
Saranac Lake
Sarasota
Saratoga Springs
Saugus
Saul
Sault Ste. Marie
Saunders
Savannah
Sawyer
Sayre
Sayreville
Scarsdale
Schenectady
Schmidt
Schneider
Schroeder
Schultz
Schuyler
Schwartz
Scotia
Scotland
Scott
Scottdale
Scottsbluff
Scranton

Seattle
Secaucus
Sedalia
Selma
Seminole
Seneca Falls
Serena
Seth
Seville
Seward
Sewickley
Sexton
Seymour
Shaker Heights
Shamokin
Shanghai
Sharon
Sharp
Sharpsburg
Sharpsville
Shaw
Shawnee
Shea
Sheboygan
Sheffield
Sheila
Shelby
Shelbyville
Sheldon
Shenandoah
Sheridan

Sherman	Somerset	Stalingrad
Sherwood	Somerville	Stamford
Shippensburg	Somersworth	Stanford
Shirley	Sonora	Stanley
Shoemaker	Sophia	State College
Shorewood	Sophronia	Statesboro
Shreveport	Sorensen	Statesville
Siam	South Africa	Staunton
Sibyl	South Amboy	Steelton
Sicily	South America	Stella
Sidney	South Bend	Stephen
Siegal	South Boston	Sterling
Siegfried	Southbridge	Steubenville
Sikeston	South Carolina	Stevens
Silas	South Dakota	Stewart
Silvanus	South Hadley	Stillwater
Silvester	Southampton	Stockholm
Silvia	Southington	Stockton
Simmons	South Orange	Stone
Simon	South River	Stoneham
Simpson	Spain	Storm Lake
Sinclair	Sparks	Stoughton
Singapore	Sparta	Stowe
Sioux City	Spartanburg	Stratford
Sioux Falls	Spencer	Straus
Skinner	Spokane	Streator
Sloan	Sprague	Stroudsburg
Smith	Springfield	Struthers
Snyder	Spring Valley	Stuart
Soloman	Stacey	Sturgeon Bay
Solvay	Stafford	Sturgis

Stuttgart	Tampa	Tifton
Sudan	Tampico	Tilda
Suffolk	Tarboro	Timothy
Sullivan	Tarentum	Tipton
Summit	Tarrytown	Titus
Sumner	Tasmania	Titusville
Sumter	Taunton	Tobiah
Sunbury	Taylor	Tokyo
Superior	Taylorville	Toledo
Susan	Teaneck	Tonawanda
Swampscott	Temple	Tony
Swansea	Tenafly	Toole
Sweden	Tennessee	Topeka
Sweetwater	Terence	Toronto
Swift	Terre Haute	Torrance
Swissvale	Terrel	Torrington
Switzerland	Terry	Toulouse
Sybil	Texarkana	Trenton
Sydney	Texas	Trieste
Sylvanus	Texas City	Trinidad
Sylvester	Thaddeus	Tripoli
Sylvia	Thalia	Troy
Syracuse	Thea	Truman
Syria	The Hague	Tuckahoe
Tabitha	Theodore	Tucson
Tacoma	Theodora	Tulane
Taft	Theresa	Tulsa
Talladega	Thomas	Tunis
Tallahassee	Thomaston	Tupelo
Tallulah	Thomasville	Turin
Tamaqua	Tiffin	Turkey

Turner
Tuscaloosa
Tuscumbia
Twin Falls
Tyler
Tyrone
Ukraine
Ulrich
Ulysses
Underhill
Underwood
Union
Union City
United Kingdom
United States
Upland
Upton
Urban
Urbana
Uriah
Ursula
Uruguay
Utah
Utica
Vail
Valdosta
Valentine
Valeria
Valley City
Valley Stream
Valparaiso

Vance
Vanderlip
Van Dyke
Van Horn
Van Wert
Vatican City
Vaughan
Venezuela
Venice
Ventnor City
Vera Cruz
Vermont
Vernon
Verona
Veronica
Vicksburg
Victor
Victoria
Villa Park
Vincennes
Vincent
Vineland
Vienna
Viola
Violet
Virgil
Virginia
Visalia
Vivian
Wabash
Waco

Waddington
Wadsworth
Wakefield
Wales
Walker
Wallace
Walla Walla
Wallingford
Wallington
Walpole
Walsenburg
Walsh
Walter
Waltham
Ward
Ware
Warren
Warrensburg
Warsaw
Warwick
Washington
Waterbury
Waterloo
Watertown
Waterville
Watervliet
Watson
Watsonville
Waukegan
Waukesha
Waupun

Wausau
Waverly
Waxahachie
Waycross
Waynesboro
Weatherford
Webb City
Webster
Welch
Wellesley
Wellington
Wellsburg
Wellston
Wellsville
Wenatchee
Wesley
West Allis
West Bend
Westbrook
West Chester
Westerly
Westfield
West Haven
West New York
Weston
West Orange
West Point
West View
West Virginia
Westwood
West York

Weymouth
Wheaton
Wheeling
White
White Plains
Whiting
Whitman
Whittier
Wichita
Wilbur
Wildwood
Wilfred
Wilkes-Barre
Wilkinsburg
Willard
William
Williamson
Williamsport
Willimantic
Williston
Willmar
Wilmerding
Wilmette
Wilmington
Wilson
Winchester
Windber
Winfield
Winifred
Winnetka
Winnipeg

Winona
Winooski
Winslow
Winsted
Winston-Salem
Winter
Winthrop
Winton
Wisconsin
Woburn
Wolf
Wood
Woodbridge
Woodbury
Woodland
Wood River
Woodruff
Woodstock
Woodward
Woonsocket
Wooster
Worcester
Worthington
Wyandotte
Wyoming
Xenia
Yakima
Yankton
Yates
Yazoo City
Yokohama

Yonkers	Ypsilanti	Yvonne
York	Yucatan	Zanesville
Young	Yugoslavia	Zenobia
Youngstown	Yuma	Zion

PART THREE
ABBREVIATIONS

Some expressions are dictated and transcribed almost exclusively in abbreviated form, such as *f.o.b.* Some expressions may be dictated and transcribed either in full or in the form of initials, such as *A.C.* or *alternating current.* The following list contains 72 such expressions with a legible shorthand outline for each set of initials.

AAF	Army Air Forces
ABC	American Broadcasting Company
A.C.	alternating current
A.D.	*anno Domini*
AEC	Atomic Energy Commission
A.F. of L.	American Federation of Labor
A.L.P.	American Labor Party
a.m.	ante meridiem
A.M.A.	American Medical Association
A.O.L.	absent over leave
APO	Army Post Office
A.S.C.A.P.	American Society of Composers, Authors, and Publishers
ASTP	Army Specialized Training Program

A.W.O.L.	absent without leave
B.B.A.	Bachelor of Business Administration
B.B.C.	British Broadcasting Corporation
B.I.S.	Bank for International Settlements
BLS	Bureau of Labor Statistics
B.t.u.	British thermal unit
CBI	China, Burma, India
CBS	Columbia Broadcasting System
cc.	cubic centimeters
c.i.f.	cost, insurance, and freight
C.I.O.	Congress of Industrial Organizations
C.O.D.	collect on delivery
C.P.A.	Certified Public Accountant
C.S.R.	Certified Shorthand Reporter
c.w.o.	cash with order
D.A.	District Attorney
D.A.R.	Daughters of the American Revolution
D.C.	direct current
D.D.S.	Doctor of Dental Surgery
DP	displaced person

DX	distance
E. & O.E.	errors and omissions excepted
Ed. D.	Doctor of Education
E.Q.	educational quotient
ERP	European Recovery Program
ETO	European Theater of Operation
FCC	Federal Communications Commission
FDIC	Federal Deposit Insurance Corporation
FM	frequency modulation
f.o.b.	free on board
FPC	Federal Power Commission
FSA	Federal Security Agency
FTC	Federal Trade Commission
GHQ	General Headquarters
HOLC	Home Owners Loan Corporation
ICC	Interstate Commerce Commission
I.L.O.	International Labor Organization
IQ	intelligence quotient
ITO	International Trade Organization
M.D.	Doctor of Medicine

NBC	National Broadcasting Company
N.E.A.	National Education Association
NLRB	National Labor Relations Board
OPA	Office of Price Administration
OSS	Office of Strategic Services
PBX	private branch exchange
p.m.	post meridiem
P.S.	postscript
P.T.A.	Parent-Teacher Association
q.v.	which see
R.F.D.	Rural Free Delivery
ROTC	Reserve Officers' Training Corps
r.p.m.	revolutions per minute
TNT	trinitrotoluene
TVA	Tennessee Valley Authority
USES	United States Employment Service
VA	Veterans' Administration
W.F.T.U.	World Federation of Trade Unions
WPA	Works Progress Administration